Parenting
by the
Spirit

PREPARING THE PARENT
(BOOK 1 OF 4)

Parenting
by the

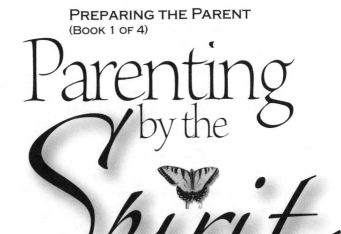

Spirit

*Yes you can
be the parent
God designed
you to be*

Sally Hohnberger

WITH TIM & JULIE CANUTESON

Pacific Press® Publishing Association
Nampa, Idaho
Oshawa, Ontario, Canada
www.pacificpress.com

Designed by Linda Griffith

Copyright © 2004 by
Pacific Press® Publishing Association
Printed in the United States of America
All Rights Reserved

Additional copies of this book are available by calling toll free 1-800-765-6955
or by visiting http://www.adventistbookcenter.com

Scripture references are taken from the King James Version
unless otherwise marked.

Library of Congress Cataloging-in-Publication Data:
Hohnberger, Sally, 1948-
Parenting by the Spirit : yes, you can be the parent God designed you
to be : raising godly children in a godless world/Sally Hohnberger.
p. cm.
ISBN 13: 978-0-8163-2031-8
ISBN 10: 0-8163-2031-4
1. Parenting—Religious aspects—Christianity.

BV4529.H62 2004
248.8'45—dc22   2004040003

06 07 08 · 5 4 3 2

Dedication

This book is dedicated to everyone who—like me—has despaired of ever being the parent God designed him or her to be; to everyone who has ever thrown up their hands in frustration.

It's dedicated to anyone who has looked at other people's offspring and vowed somehow not to make the same mistakes.

It's dedicated to every parent—past, present, and future—with a prayer that you will take its principles and, through God's power, gain a miracle of transformation in your own heart and then in the hearts of your children.

Contents

Preface

Initially, the idea for this book began with a number of people expressing a need for a child-rearing book that would take them step by step through the learning process. They suggested I should write such a book, little knowing how difficult it is for me to write even a four-page article! The time it takes me to write is incredible. I tend to be excessive with words, and it costs me much time, effort, and energy to go back and cut to be concise. The task of writing a book seemed not just monumental, but impossible! So for some time I dismissed these requests. I chalked them up to human nature just expecting me to write a book because I'm married to Jim. But I knew I needed to consult God about this. At the same time I certainly hoped He wasn't calling me to write a book!

So I went to the Lord and said, "What is Your will in this matter? Do you want me to write a book? I will try—but only if I'm convinced the call is from You! I know You can empower me for the task although it goes against my every inclination. Can you give me something to confirm Your will to me?"

And God impressed on my heart, "*Sally, I want you to start writing that book.*"

"But Lord, who am I? Sure, I love helping people, but it has always been one-on-one. You've developed a gift in me to reach out and touch the hearts of children and youth and make You real to them. But, Lord, how do I bring this across effectively in print?"

"*Sally, you have successfully raised two fine, young men to follow Jesus as their Lord—and you still question whether you are qualified? As you raised these boys, you consistently put their education and character development first and foremost. You held My hand, and I directed your steps. This is the secret to success for anyone! Yes, you have made mistakes, yet you have cooperated to correct them in Me. You have helped many to gain a vision of what parenting truly is—and what it isn't. You can share your experiences with them. Tell the people how I have helped you over each hurdle in life. Tell them I'd love to help them in the management of their children and home life, too. Make religion and walking with Me practical to them from your life story. I will be with you!"*

And so I have attempted to do just that. I am not the pattern to follow. Jesus Christ is the one and only Pattern. In the following pages, I have tried, with my hand in Christ's, to make living the Christian life practical, through the indwelling of His presence guiding and directing us. Child rearing is an awesome responsibility that we cannot accomplish without Him. True parenting is getting in touch with the hearts of our children to connect their minds with Christ's so that they may be empowered to perform the otherwise impossible task of living the Christian life against their flesh.

The book you hold in your hands is the first book in a proposed series of four on true child rearing. This book is designed to connect you to a personal God in order to be empowered to be the parent you desire to be.

On the horizon, I plan three additional books which will comprise a very practical series on parenting. One book will deal specifically with our precious infants, one with our moldable children, and one with our soon-to-be-adult youth. Each book will address practical steps in how to win them and bring them to Christ. The experience with Christ demonstrated in these books holds forth the key to making a success no matter what age your children are.

My prayer is that we will each commit ourselves to God to become instruments in His hand to raise our children to serve a powerful God in a powerful way!

Chapter 1

EMBRACING THE WORK

"We shall be like him" (1 John 3:2).

The home I grew up in was indelibly marked by the mental illness and violent rages of my stepfather. My mother stayed with him mostly out of fear, and it was not unheard of for the police to be involved in our domestic situation. Despite these difficult circumstances, I never knew depression until I had become a professed Christian with two small children. As a young Christian mother, I had high ideals and lofty goals, but reality fell far short of all my desires and plans.

I had just put my baby, Andrew, down for his nap and was on the phone with a friend when I discovered two-year-old Matthew throwing dog food all over the dining room floor! Excusing myself from the phone, I promptly confronted my little mischief-maker with my hands on my hips. The look in my eyes clearly told him my displeasure. And if that wasn't enough, my body language, the deep sigh, and the tone of my voice emphasized my frustration.

"Matthew, pick up the dog food immediately!" I commanded.

Matthew looked away and started playing with the dog food remaining in the dish.

"Matthew, pick up that dog food right now!"

No response. My mind whirled as I wondered what I should be doing. Ephesians 6:1 came to mind: "Children, obey your parents." Matthew simply *must* obey me; Jesus wanted him to. I remembered Abraham and how he commanded his household after him. "That's it," I told myself, "I must be too soft! If I were firmer, like Abraham, my two-year-old would obey me." I didn't understand, then, that Satan can use Scripture to seduce us into wrong pathways—just as he tried to do with Jesus Himself. Meanwhile, Matthew dawdled at the dog's dish, unmoved by my commands.

His unyielding spirit reigned even after my third, fourth, and fifth commands, followed with spankings each time. Oh, he went through the motions, but he picked up only a handful of dog food, and that against his will. My own spirit grew more angry and harsh as I tried everything I could think of to *make* him obey, but this, too, ended in absolute failure. Despair swept over me, and I left Matthew crying in his bedroom. I was ashamed of my failure to gain obedience—and even more ashamed of my loss of self-control.

I didn't understand why my method of discipline wasn't working. Hadn't I reproved and corrected, applying the rod like the Bible said I should? But where was the obedience?

I didn't know it then, but I was following my own reasoning—doing what was right in "mine own eyes," as the Scripture calls it. I didn't know anything else. I wanted Christ to lead me, but I was following my own inclinations. As a result, Satan ruled in my life! One master or the other always rules us, and my attitude revealed clearly the reflection of the evil one.

I thought the problem was Matthew, not I. Since Eden, human beings have always blamed others for *their own* failures. Sometimes, we even blame God! Have you done it? I have. I had been trying to do what God's Word said, but I was destined to fail because I was trying to do so in my own power.

"Lord, what have I done! What can I do to make it right?" The tears streamed down my cheeks, and remorse burned within me. I looked at my hands, remembering how they had just spanked Matthew so unreasonably. I felt so ashamed, I sat on them, as if putting them out of sight could make the memory go away. I began to understand how one could so easily go from discipline to abuse. This had been just too close, and it frightened me! "Mercy, Lord!" I prayed. I tuned my ears toward heaven desperately hoping for an answer, but not really expecting one. I dared not yield to this spirit again.

Then this thought came clearly into my mind: *"You left out the main ingredient in your discipline."*

This had to be God speaking through my conscience, but I felt too unworthy for communication with God. "I did *what?*" I listened again, unsure what to expect. This experience was too new to be my imagination and too practical to be a dream.

"Sally, you left out the love in your discipline. You need to balance firmness with love—not just your love, but My love. Let Me direct your steps so that we can work cooperatively to win the heart of your child. You can't gain true inward obedience from your child using harshness and anger, no matter how hard you try or how right you may be. You can drive in devils with this method, but you can't drive them out. No spanking will change his heart unless you love him with My divine love and he knows that you love him that way."

"Lord, I'm making a mess of raising my children! I want to do it right, but I'm so depressed I'm ready to give up. Maybe someone else would do a better job of raising them."

"Sally, I don't need anyone else to raise your children. I need you! I want you to learn how to walk and talk with Me in your child rearing. I'll teach you. All I need is your hand continually in Mine and your ear listening for My instructions. If you follow My directions, you can walk with me like Enoch did. Do you want to?"

"Oh yes, I want to. But how can I ever make it up to Matthew for my harshness? Will he ever love me again? I was so angry with him, and now I see it wasn't even his fault. I was the problem, not him."

"I am your Helper in trouble. I will never leave you or forsake you. If you will get Matthew right now, and tell him you are sorry, I will be with you and lead you in obtaining what you desire."

My emotions pushed me to doubt. "Is this really God speaking in my thoughts?" I wondered. I wanted to act on the directions God had given, but that meant I would have to go against my feelings and emotions. It was terribly hard to do so. But I believed this was God speaking to me. So I chose to act. I walked resolutely to Matthew's room.

My courage nearly failed when I entered his room and saw him run to hide in the farthest corner. I picked him up and held him, but he squirmed in my arms to get down. I sensed that my own precious son was afraid of me! I sat down in a chair and told him how sorry I was. "I will never spank you that way again. I promise!" I said, waiting for some type of magical transformation. You see, I expected a quick, easy solution with God leading, so it came as a shock when his fear turned to anger and he began beating on my chest with his little fists. The feelings of guilt and helplessness welled up even more because I felt I deserved his retaliation.

"Lord, there's no hope for me! He'll never forgive me!" I cried out in despair. I listened, but there was no voice from on high, commanding me to take a certain action. No new thoughts came to my mind—just the conviction to follow my God-led heart. Again I apologized to Matthew and asked him to forgive me. I assured him that I loved him, and this time his eyes met mine. His fists slowed to a halt. His little mind was being led of God to love and trust again. I could sense it intuitively. His icy disposition with all the anger and hatred melted before my eyes. It was a miraculous moment.

Almost before I knew it, his arms were around my neck. His eyes— and more importantly, his heart—were filled with love from above. My son had forgiven me! Now I cried again, but this time with tears of joy. God had spoken to me when I was the least worthy and simply told me what to do. I did it, and it worked! This concept was so new to me that I struggled to grasp it. "Why didn't I ask for His wisdom in the beginning?" I questioned myself.

In a few minutes, our emotions settled down, and I was impressed of God to continue the course I had started and carry it through to its conclusion. I walked Matthew back into the dining room and pointed to the dog's dish. This time there were no hands on my hips, commands, or anger. I didn't even speak. I just pointed. Matthew smiled and diligently picked up all the dog food, putting it back in the dish. Shilo, our Britanny Spaniel, trotted beside him, picking up too, although his contributions were not returned to the dish!

This was one of my first exposures to true heart surrender, a memorable glimpse of true, willing obedience and a valuable insight into what my child could be like if he and I had willing dispositions and were being led of God. All I had done was to ask God what to do, listen, and then do what He said, even though it went against the tide of my emotions. The solution to my parenting dilemmas couldn't be that easy. Or could it?

Many unanswered questions swirled through my mind over the next several days. Could God give me the wisdom He gave Solomon to judge the misdemeanors of my children? I struggled with balancing the issues of justice and mercy. Quickly, it seemed, I forgot this new experience and tried again to do it all myself—that is, I tried to do what God said I should do—without Him. But again I failed to bring my boys to a truehearted obedience. "Why doesn't this work?" I would complain bitterly when confronted once again with failure. "I must not be consistent enough, or maybe I don't pray enough. Firmness, yes, that's it. I must not be firm enough." Then, once more, I'd give way to harshness and anger when I corrected the boys, although I was careful never, never again to allow myself to lose control as before.

I did the things I did simply because I didn't know what else to do. It didn't work. My methods didn't yield the results I desired, but to do nothing and allow my children to come up like weeds seemed criminal! I didn't know what to do; I hated being a mother *this way*!

I called my best friend and spiritual mentor, Edith. It was embarrassing, but I confessed, "I'm really concerned about myself. God must hate me. I'm so unworthy to be called a Christian. Edith, I hate my children!! How can I teach anyone to be like Jesus when I don't know how to be Christlike myself?"

"Oh, you don't hate your children, Sally! You're just frustrated! Children don't always obey; it's a part of life. You expect too much of yourself."

"No Edith," I tried to explain, "there is something really wrong. In my heart I have hatred toward my children—not simply frustration. What can I do about it?"

"Listen Sally, parenting is tough work, and you're doing a good job. Your boys are the best-behaved boys in church."

Bless her heart, she was trying to encourage me, trying to lift me up, but missing the fact that I was really in trouble, not so much because I was having problems with my kids, but because I was disconnected from God.

I felt desperate. "She doesn't understand how serious this is," I told myself. "I'm not explaining it well enough. God says hatred is murder. I was hoping that of all people, she could help me. I'll try calling Anne. Maybe she will understand me."

"Sally," Anne answered when I called, "what's the matter? Are you all right? You don't sound too good."

"Anne, I'm not all right. Listen, I know it sounds horrible, but I hate my children! No, I'm not joking. I'm really serious. What am I to do?"

"Oh Sally, you don't hate your children," she soothed. "You love children! You take care of my children and everyone else's, for that matter, and you love them all. Why, you teach them about Jesus, what is good, and how to pray. You don't hate your children!"

"Yes, Anne, I do. I'm very disturbed about this, and I have to find answers. I can't go on like this. I've tried to raise my children to do right and follow God. I'm depressed because I can't do it. I just can't!"

Anne tried, but she didn't understand either, which further convinced me that I was inferior as a parent. After all, nobody else had these kinds of feelings toward their children.

That night when Jim came home, I was all prepared to talk with him about my problem over supper. He had always been my helper. "He's so good at finding solutions; I know he will tell me just what to do," I comforted myself.

"Jim, I'm so frustrated," I began nearly in tears. "I'm trying to be a good mother and teach the boys to obey, but I'm just not doing a good job."

"What's the problem?" he muttered in an irritated voice.

"Well, I can't get Matthew to obey me," I wailed, telling a short version of the dog food incident.

I longed for sympathy and understanding, but Jim's face registered frustration, "Sally, Matthew's only two years old. Come on! Just make him obey you! You're bigger and stronger than he is; just do it! This conversation is ridiculous!"

I was frustrated and hurt. No one seemed to understand just how seriously I viewed this problem. Even Jim wasn't able to help me. He didn't perceive the crisis I was in.

I walked down the lane to the lake. As I took in the peaceful setting, my mind raced. In desperation, I started talking to God. "Lord, this is serious stuff. My friends don't understand! They tell me I'm good, and I know I'm not. My husband thinks I'm ridiculous because I can't get our son to obey in a simple situation. He doesn't know that it was a two-hour battle of the wills. I don't know what to do. I am at the end of my rope, and I don't deserve to come to You. But no one else will listen. Other mothers don't have this problem. I'm the only one." I was filled with self-pity.

Then God spoke plainly to me, just like before. It was not an audible voice; He spoke through impressions in my thoughts, bringing me ideas that I knew didn't originate with me, ideas that spoke to the deepest needs of my heart. *"Sally, I love you. Come to Me with your problems and difficulties. You can't change unless you come to Me. You need My divine power to re-create you. I don't want to just help you; I want to change you on the inside and then give you My wisdom to direct your steps. Mothers have a special place in My heart, and I always want to help mothers with their children. Do you remember the text you have been memorizing this week?"*

It came to mind quickly: "Call upon me in the day of trouble; I will deliver thee, and thou shalt glorify me" (Psalm 50:15). Oh how I needed to be delivered from the wrong kind of parenting, from giving way to harshness and anger, wielding autocratic rule, and being cold and dictatorial. "I'm in a big mess, Lord," I confessed. "I've fallen into the pit of despair again, and it's just getting deeper and more hopeless each time I fall back into it."

My problem was not that I didn't believe what God was sharing with me. My problem was that my oft-repeated failures had robbed me of confidence in my ability to actually do what God might tell me to do. "I'm glad for Your willingness to help me," I continued. "I wish I understood how to bring my children to truehearted obedience, but for now I'm much more concerned over the fact that I feel hatred toward my children. What am I to do?"

"Give Me those hateful feelings. You fail so often because you cannot control your impulses or your emotions as you want. But here is the good news, Sally—I can! When you give Me your wrong thoughts or feelings, I will cleanse them and return them to you purified."

My thoughts raced. Could this be true? "Lord, how do I give you something, like feelings, that aren't tangible?"

"You can choose whom you will serve. Do you remember the text you read in 1 Peter 5:7, 'Casting all your care upon him; for He careth for you'? That is what I am inviting you to do. Sally, it's like casting a stone into the lake. You no longer have the stone, do you? When you cast your hateful feelings to Me, so I can subdue them for you, I'll keep them as long as you don't try to take them back. Try Me!"

"Okay, Lord, here are my hateful feelings. I can't change them, but I believe You can. I'm looking to your strength and not to my weakness. I cast them on You." I waited, examining my heart, but nothing seemed any different. "Why do I still feel them, Lord? Didn't I give them to You?"

"Yes, you gave them. The feelings may remain for a while after you choose to give them up. That is why salvation is a work of faith. A step of faith is one that is not seen, and yet is believed. Faith is not sight, feelings, or emotions. It is choosing to believe what My Word says over and above the feelings that want to overwhelm and control you. Sally, act as though the feelings of hatred are gone already. Faith is also an action, isn't it? Remember when you first came to Me and confessed your sins, yet you didn't feel forgiven? I took you to 1 John 1:9 and told you not to judge by your feelings, but by what My Word says. And when you did that, you stepped

into the experience of forgiveness and tasted My peace, didn't you?"

"Yes I did. The feelings of sorrow and guilt stayed around a while. It will probably be the same this time." I reasoned. "Let me recall, how long did it take for them to disappear?"

"No, don't set up that kind of a pattern to judge by. It may not always be that way. You see, I can miraculously take away wrong feelings instantly or slowly. You must trust Me, not a method! I know what you most need, and it is your work to cultivate trust in Me whether the feelings remain a long time or short. Let My Holy Spirit work in you, instead of expecting the Holy Spirit to work your way. Give Me your wrong thoughts and feelings. If they return, yield them again, and repeat this process until they are fully gone. In Me, you need not be under the control of these feelings any longer. Abide in Me until your redemption is complete."

"When will I know it's complete?"

"You will know; I will make you aware."

"Okay, I've given You my hate." I envisioned myself throwing a stone in the lake and thought, I don't have it any more—Jesus does! "Now what would You have me to do?"

"Sally, have you ever noticed that when someone moves out of a house and leaves it vacant, before long the worst elements of society occupy the vacated property and bring it into terrible condition? The same thing happens in the human mind. You must not leave vacant the space those feelings used to occupy. The replacement principle is not leaving the house empty for devils to come and fill. Put in the opposite thoughts and feelings. What would those be?"

God is a good teacher He always encourages me to reason from cause to effect. So I thought about His question for a moment and answered, "Well the opposite of hate is love."

"You have reasoned well, Sally. You need to think loving thoughts toward your offending son."

"Well . . . well . . ." I stammered. "I can't think of a thing. I can think of a lot of things that I don't like, but nothing good! I'm really trying, Lord, but it's like my mind is stuck in a rut."

"Sally, this is the hold sin has on you. As you rehearse the faults of your children, those faults grow bigger, and you get stuck in a rut. But more importantly, this habit separates you from Me because soon only the negative seems real. Your way out is to obey Me, trust in My strength, and seek to do My will. Like the eagle, you must break through the dark clouds, believing that the sun is on the other side. Now I'll get you started thinking good things about your son. He's a generous child, isn't he?"

"Oh yes, it's one of his strongest attributes. I had forgotten about it amidst all the rubbish I was thinking and feeling." Suddenly, like a dam bursting, the positive thoughts started to pour out! "He is thoughtful with his affectionate hugs, a real joy to be around. His smile is charming; his laugh infectious."

And so I got started. I felt like the servant filling my water pots with water at the wedding feast in Cana, waiting for Jesus to turn it into wine. It had seemed impossible, but in a relatively short time, my thoughts, attended by God's grace, had flowed into my feelings, and true love from the inside was bubbling out toward my children, obvious to all. I knew God had performed a miracle in me. Hate was slain and love now reigned! Praise God! He changed my water into the sweetest grape juice, and it was sweetly transforming my thoughts, feelings, and emotions. My family recognized and appreciated the joy, love, and enthusiasm that flowed out of me to grace our home again.

In Jesus, I learned that I could love my son again. In Jesus, my son learned he could forgive me. What a joy! I knew God had worked His redemption in *me!* In Christ I was enabled to walk successfully against the pull of my flesh in the opposite direction.

In looking back on this experience, I began to understand why I had never known depression until I was a professed Christian trying to live by godly principles. When I was just a nominal Christian floating through life, Satan left me alone. I was no threat to him. But when I determined to be a follower of Christ and tried to live what I read in God's Word, I found Satan opposing my way—just as Scripture says. "We wrestle not against flesh and blood, but against principalities, against powers, against the rulers of the darkness of this world" (Ephesians 6:12).

I had erred in child rearing by trying to obey God through my human willpower and reason alone, without any connection or power from God to direct my ways. I didn't realize that my child's will wasn't the only force I was combating. Satan easily thwarted my efforts by inspiring my child to disobey, and in so doing, he pushed those buttons in me that stirred my emotions and made me faultfinding and angry.

Many parents, who have never had a genuine relationship with God, are asking their children to "be good" and fight against Satan without a vital connection with Jesus. How can our children war against powers and principalities without Christ? They can't! We are asking them to do the impossible, and then labeling them rebellious and disobedient when they fail. How crazy we are to send our child to battle with Satan alone, unaided by Divinity!

Embracing the work is *first* embracing Christ. It's letting Him have all of me—the good, the bad, and the ugly. It's letting Him put His loving, redeeming arms around me. It's learning to trust God and to no longer fear the changes He may ask me to make.

Embracing the work is doing my part—that which God cannot do for me. My part is to seek God, and to surrender to His will. This means putting all my energies in gear to walk holding His hand. Oh, what a fearful embrace this is when we go in opposition to our self-driven thoughts, feelings, and emotions! But, oh, what a joyful embrace it becomes when we experience Christ's miraculous transformation on this level!

Embracing the work is an admission that my way of parenting isn't working and that I am looking to Christ for the new approach, the new heart, the new attitude I need in order to successfully get my child to cooperate and embrace Christ. Both parent and child need Christ in order to change.

Embracing the work begins with the sincere desire to make things different. You must have that God-given desire or you would never have opened this book. It's my wish to provide you information that is practical. I want to give you the eagle's eye view of what parenting is—the big picture—as well as relate to you down at ground level, in the day-to-day battles where the problems of life often make it easy to lose sight of our overall goal.

You will hear a lot about dealing with self-will in this book because we cannot hope to deal with our child's self-will unless we have learned to deal with our own.

You'll find in this book organized information, but you will not find a "method" for child rearing. Every child is a unique individual, and the "method" that works for one may not be the perfect solution for another. But if we learn to depend upon God to direct our discipline and training, we will find success.

In Christ, our efforts will find success no matter how difficult the situation! God wants us to embrace Divinity to obey Him, to serve Him above our flesh, our senses, our emotions, or our selfish thoughts that pull us in the opposite direction.

His grace is sufficient. It's waiting for you. Come with me and explore a vital, new way to parent!

THE LONE EMBRACE
A SPECIAL WORD OF ENCOURAGEMENT FOR SINGLE PARENTS

The question often comes up: "Do these principles work for single parents?"

The answer is a decided "yes"—and "no." Perhaps in most cases the best answer is, "It depends." It depends upon the *individual* just as much as it does in the two-parent home. The child's destiny until old enough to form an independent relationship with God is largely in the hands of the parent, who either *is or isn't* willing to die to self that the child may be helped to understand how to come to God. If the single parent desires that experience badly enough to place it high on the priority list, then he or she can do a job at least equal to, if not superior to, many two-parent homes. This doesn't mean the single parent faces an easy task. Unquestionably, it is much harder for the single parent to do his or her part with God simply because there is no one to help, no "relief shift."

To offset the single parent disadvantage, God makes a precious promise to you. He promises to be a father to the fatherless (see Psalm 68:5). Jesus is willing to fulfill the role of the missing spouse, be it a husband or a wife. If you avail yourself of this gift, you can't lose. You'll have to work hard and remain sensitive to God's leading moment by moment, but the evidences of His care will bring you joy and peace. To be God led, you'll have to give up your independence, but that will enable you to be successful in eternal things. The joy will outweigh the hardness of the way. He can be more real to you in your situation than when He walked with his disciples on earth. God offers this close companionship to you.

Others in your life may have taken advantage of you, hurt you, or been unfaithful. God will be loyal, faithful, and always care for you. Give yourself time with Him and be vulnerable to Him, and you will learn to trust Him like no one else, for He is trustworthy.

The challenge for you, if you are a single parent, is time—time to yield yourself to God, time that seems at a premium amid earning a living, endless household tasks, and the needs and activities of your children. Yet no other single thing you do will yield such results in your home as managing your time to achieve the goal of self-surrender to God, and subsequently, the surrender of your child.

The fact that you have more demands on your time means you must be scheduled, a subject that we will deal with in more detail later. It means that your priority must be this experience with God and that other things will have to be sacrificed. I have found that no matter how busy I am, if I want to do something badly enough, I can find the time.

THE MARY PRINCIPLE

"And Mary said, Behold the handmaid of the Lord; be it unto me according to thy word" (Luke 1:38).

Engaged! Betrothed! These words were the romantic dream of every girl in the village, and doubtless, Mary felt the same emotional stirrings as any prospective bride whose love has backed his feelings with a firm commitment to their future wedding. *Joseph, her dear Joseph!* The very thought of him caused her heart to skip a beat, and such overwhelming love poured from the depths of her being that she could hardly contain it. She had started dreaming of her own home and being just the wife Joseph needed. Her friends playfully teased her with just a touch of envy, and the whole family looked forward to the celebration.

In the formalized betrothal, Mary left her youth behind even though the marriage had not yet occurred. She gained status in the community, which supported and encouraged such unions as a way to create a secure future. Once publicly sanctioned, the engagement had official status and could be broken only through a writ of divorcement. Only rarely did this happen, but when it did, it was almost always scandalous. Generally, an otherwise nice girl would be found with child. Then angry denouncements followed, heaped on the poor woman by her betrothed, his family, even her friends—while the man who had seduced her would all too often just disappear from her life. Usually she'd have to leave the village, and rumors would eventually bring the news that she had gone to live with distant relatives in the hill country where at last she had married a man of poor social standing who didn't object to receiving damaged goods. Mary would have shuddered with horror at the thought; it was every girl's nightmare to be thus disgraced. Of course, Mary had no such worries, for she had known no man. Her purity was unquestioned.

Mary had no idea her life was about to radically change, that an angel of God would appear to her with the shocking news that God had chosen *her* to be the mother of the Messiah, the Savior and King of Israel. Every woman born of Abraham's line desired this destiny, but how few, if any, had thought of the problems this might bring, rather than the glory sure to be theirs. Now as the heavenly messenger stood before her, these troubles may have crossed Mary's mind. But if so, they faded before the vision of God's will. It seems clear that Mary had cultivated the habit of yielding her desires to the revealed will of God. No wonder Joseph fell in love with her!

Understandably baffled, Mary questioned the angel about the apparent impossibility of her conceiving. Is the child to result from her future union with Joseph? The angel patiently explains that this Child will result from divine intervention and therefore He would be called the Son of God.

Mary is shocked. How would we react? Probably with disbelief, laughter, or even doubt. But for Mary, the response was acceptance. "Behold the handmaid of the Lord; be it unto me according to thy word" (Luke 1:38). There was no hesitancy, thinking about what others would think of her—pregnant and unwed.

Mary was willing to be completely led by God, and yet, she was very human. She immediately left for Elizabeth's home to verify, as much as possible, the angel's story that her kinswoman, Elizabeth, had miraculously conceived and thus encourage her own faith. Staying with Elizabeth until after the birth of John, Mary returned to her home and her beloved Joseph after an absence of three or four months. She had to try to explain to her betrothed that she was pregnant, that she hadn't been unfaithful and was still a virgin, that an angel had appeared to her, and that she was to be the mother of the Promised One, the Messiah. I would rather try to sell ice to Eskimos!

I am sure Joseph listened, but it was all just too far-fetched. Mary, *his* Mary, had gone off and gotten pregnant. He couldn't understand why, but hurt as he was, he made up his mind to end the engagement as quietly as possible. Joseph was a man of character and principle. God respected this man who was led by principle and sent Joseph a message, telling him not to fear to take Mary as his wife, for the whole story she had told him was true.

Now Joseph faced a choice. If he obeyed God, many would think the child was his; his reputation would suffer. Yet he went forward with his plans to be married, and in so doing he proved himself worthy to become the earthly father of our Lord. He and Mary both understood something few of us understand today in our relationship with God. Elizabeth's child verbalized it years afterward, when he was known throughout the nation as John the Baptist: "He [Jesus] must increase, but I must decrease" (John 3:30).

It's a privilege to follow God and be misunderstood. We can do right, and others may misrepresent us, yet God is still leading. Will we, like Mary and Joseph, follow God's lead, discerning His will?

Successful parenting is more than providing for our children, more than just loving them. Successful parenting is raising them to be like Jesus. And to do that, we must have Mary's attitude of "Whatever you say, Lord, I will do." This attitude involves the discipline to learn to recognize God's voice to our souls. It involves the cultivated desire to pray and wait upon God. And it involves realizing the experience John the Baptist spoke of, in which self is put away and Christ is allowed to shine increasingly through our actions and expression. We must gain this experience for ourselves. It isn't something one can give to another. That is why this is not a typical how-to book. The parenting I want to share with you in this book is not a concept as much as it is an experience with Jesus—letting Him lead and cooperating with Him. This was how Mary became a tool in God's hand to raise Jesus. She was a success because she chose the attitude of being only an instrument in God's hand to do His will.

How does this work in a practical real-life setting? Let's take a look.

When Jim and I married, we immediately bought a house we could barely afford and moved into an even nicer home after a few years. I worked as an RN at a kidney dialysis center for a number of years. I was twenty-eight, pregnant with our first child, and life was wonderful.

We were proud and delighted when Matthew was born. I was looking forward to returning to work after my six weeks of maternity leave. I had a fine baby sitter picked out. Jim and I had just become Bible-believing Christians. I still remember reading, "I will instruct thee and teach thee in the way which thou shalt go" (Psalm 32:8). The text seemed so personal, so close, but we didn't understand what it meant in a practical way.

"Lord," I prayed one morning on my way to work, "I am so delighted with my job. Why, I can talk with my patients about spiritual issues and all the things that concern them about death and dying. As you open the way, I can share with my patients all that I'm learning from my Bible. I'm so happy. You've even provided me the best baby sitter I could have, the church-school teacher's wife. Matthew will be well cared for, taught Christian principles, and she'll even pray with him!"

Then a new thought wandered into my consciousness—a thought so new and foreign that I knew God prompted it for my contemplation: *"Will Matthew learn her view of Christianity or yours?"*

"Well hers, of course. But she's been raised a Christian and knows You better than I do, a brand new convert. Why, she's teaching me! Surely, this is Your will, Lord—or is it?"

I couldn't recall ever asking God about our plans. Everything had been working out so perfectly, there hadn't seemed to be any reason to question whether He was blessing—until now. I can't describe the uncertainty that suddenly rose in my heart. But God had more for me to think about.

"Do you really want the caregiver instilling her values in your son?" The Lord asked.

"Yes. Well . . . no. Then again, yes, it's okay," I struggled to reassure myself. From deep within my heart, desires were welling up that I didn't even know I had. The wish to claim my rightful place and position as

Matthew's mother surged to the top. "No!" I declared, "I don't want that! I want him to have my views and Jim's. Oh Lord, I don't know what to think!"

"Did Mary raise Jesus or did another?"

"Mary did. Does that mean raising Matthew is my responsibility, Lord?" My thoughts were in turmoil. Which were from God? Were some from Satan? How could I know? I sensed God was calling me to be a mother, not a dialysis nurse.

Confusion generally results when God's will confronts us and it opposes our desires or plans. Often this leads us to a very vital question: How can I know God's will? Our answer will have profound implications for our future lives. If we ask that question, honestly seeking God, we are standing at the very portals of heaven, close enough to reach over the gulf and gain the empowering wisdom of the King of kings. If we ask it as an expression of doubt, we are placing ourselves in a position where Heaven is unable to help us.

The conflict between my plans and God's will affected my emotions and thoughts so much that my reasoning became like a two-headed animal, trying to go in opposite directions. Finances loomed in front of me. That was the main reason I couldn't stay home! Yet the importance of being a mother and raising my son clamored to be heard as well. But this new idea just didn't fit into *our* plans.

Over the next six months, Jim and I talked endlessly about this issue, prayed about it fervently, searched our Bibles for information, counseled with others, and finally made the fearful decision that I would stay home to be the mother God was calling me to be! There was absolutely no way we could afford for me to not work as a nurse, but we felt that God was asking me to stay home—and at least we had to try it. We made a decision based on faith. It seemed impossible, yet we decided that if this was what Jesus wanted us to do, all our wisdom was foolishness compared to God's wisdom, and we chose to trust Him.

We didn't understand the Mary Principle as we do today, but we were following it the best we knew how. "Be it unto me according to thy word" (Luke 1:38). I didn't yet comprehend how thorough God's work would be in my heart. My great love for nursing waned while my longing to be home to raise my son ascended. Just how God changes those things in us, I don't understand. I think we sometimes get in trouble when we try to explain everything God does in neat theological terms our finite minds can understand. After all, His ways are "past finding out" (Romans 11:33). It was a truly mysterious inner work, and I am so grateful He did it, even if I can't fully explain it.

God called me to stay home and give Matthew our religious beliefs and experience. I thought it was going to be a piece of cake. Caring for a baby would be such a simple task. Was I ever mistaken! If we could talk to Mary, I believe she would say the same thing regarding raising Jesus. As parents, we all learn on the job. She, too, must have encountered sorrows, perplexities, and uncertainty in her child rearing.

Each day I said a cheery Goodbye to Jim as he went off to work and then went to play a while with my darling Matthew. Of course, he was delighted to have me involved with him, but I had trouble the very first day. When I tried to get a few household tasks done and left Matthew in the living room, he wailed. "Oh well, it will soon be time to feed him and put him down for his morning nap," I told myself, as I rushed back to comfort him. Only Matthew decided he wasn't going to take a nap.

"I thought babies slept a lot. Maybe he needs to be more tired." So I let him stay up and entertained him. I didn't know it then, but I was setting up a pattern of behavior that we would have to struggle for years to undo! I soon found that Matthew wanted to be with me *all* the time, wherever I went. I made the mistake of giving him what he cried for, partly because I felt guilty for leaving him those months while I struggled to make up my mind. The other problem was Jim. In my heart, I really thought I ought to let Matthew cry it out at night, but Jim couldn't stand the endless crying, not even for fifteen minutes! So I would get up as soon as the baby cried. I was torn between my child's needs and my husband's needs. I honestly didn't know what to do.

Weeks and months continued in a similar fashion. I began to resent not having any time to myself, always having to entertain this baby, who, I felt, used misbehavior to force me into doing what *he* wanted. I soon found myself wishing I was back at the dialysis center. Little did I know that such struggles are the lot of all who embrace the Mary Principle.

I wasn't finding parenting to be the pleasant, fulfilling task God intended it to be. Yes, God intended parenting to be enjoyable, but most of us don't find it that way because we don't understand our position before God. I was trying to do everything God said in His Word about child rearing, asking Him to bless my efforts, but I was trying to do it all *myself*, apart from Christ. Jesus needed to lead, but I wouldn't get out of the way. I was extremely frustrated; yet, I did not turn to God because I simply didn't think I needed Him. Child rearing was my job.

Catering to your infant like I catered to Matthew's every whim is a *huge* mistake that will cost you much heartache now and in the future. The problem is that your infant shares the same heritage you and I do as sinners. The flesh with which we are born wants its own way, and wants it now! The unsurrendered human heart can never be satisfied. No matter how many concessions you make to your child's wants, he will never be truly happy, only more controlling and peevish. Therefore, the most loving thing you can do for your child is to teach him, from the earliest age, habits of self-control and how to deny the demands of the sinful nature by submitting to the parent and to God. It means giving him what is good for him instead of what he wants and demands. It means consistency, regularity, and being under the influence of the Holy Spirit. It means letting God be in control.

Before we go on, I want to provide a bit of balance. Always giving in to your child isn't the right way, but neither is always denying him. Just as in our personal walk with God, so as we travel the road of child rearing, there is a ditch on either side—the ditch of overdoing and the ditch of underdoing. Satan doesn't care which ditch we fall into as long as we go to one extreme or the other. God wants to keep us balanced in the middle. Sometimes babies are fussy and need to be rocked and cuddled for a time. Other times that is not the right solution. As we learn to let God be the pilot, we will consult Him and lean on His wisdom to know what to do.

The difficulties in rearing our children after God's character are a motivating force turning us to God to sort out the answers and to gain the experience of a personal God directing our steps. There are trials and difficulties that accompany these changes. Not everyone will agree with our course of action. We all need the courage and independence to follow Christ as did Mary. There are some attending problems that come when we follow God rather than men.

I read "Children, obey your parents" (Ephesians 6:1) and sensed I should be teaching my baby to obey even before he could reason. So with a thimble full of knowledge, I tried and tried, in and of myself, to get Matthew to go to bed, not to cry—and sometimes it worked, but usually it failed. Who was winning? Matthew was. I was obeying my son. God was not in charge; I was. But praise the Lord, Christ was able to pilot me out of my wrong concepts!

"Sally you need to read Ephesians 6:1 more closely. You're missing something."

"Lord, it reads, 'Children, obey your parents *in the Lord.*'" Wow! As often as I had read this text, I had never caught those last three words before—*"in the Lord."* "So what does it mean, 'in the Lord'"?

"It means to be like Mary. Self-will wasn't ruling Mary's life; she held herself willing to do whatever I asked of her, whether it was comfortable or not. 'In the Lord' means that I'm the Pilot instructing you—the copilot—what to do next. It's hearing and obeying My Spirit."

I hadn't been "in the Lord"! I'd been trying to be in charge, making all the decisions. I wasn't asking God for help or seeking His way. I was just following my own reasoning. To be a parent "in the Lord" doesn't just happen; it requires us to develop a distrust of our wisdom and to seek earnestly to know how to let Jesus pilot us.

Here is how to begin. No matter how sure you are about what needs to be done, sincerely seek God's will in every interaction with your child. God is there by your side ready to help you, so ask Him! Say, "Lord, how would You respond in this situation if You were me? How can I get my child's heart into your hands so that your Holy Spirit can make his or her disposition mild and like Yours?"

Don't repeat my mistakes. Only long after the fact did I begin to understand why I failed in those early years in spite of all my good intentions. I failed because I thought my job was to change my child rather than to let God use me as His instrument to bring my child to Him to be changed. You see, when I sat up with Matthew for hours, trying to get him to sleep until he finally got tired and gave in, I didn't win. He didn't obey me; I obeyed him! What a revelation it was to me when I realized that God never intended me to teach my child to obey on my own! That I couldn't do it without Him. That's why I failed—I was trying to raise my child without relying on God. And if you're failing at rearing your child today, that's likely the reason for you as well.

If we practice being like Mary and say, "Be it unto me according to thy word" (Luke 1:38), it will save us a lot of heartache in the end. As we stepped out in faith, some interesting things began to happen. Amazingly, Jim's business prospered and soon more than replaced my income. In choosing to stay at home and raise my child, I had to learn new attitudes and priorities, and each one brought its own struggles and problems—but blessings in the end. As I look back at the results, I'm so glad I chose to stay at home. God did know best!

In my mind's eye, I can see the heartache we would be experiencing now if we had stayed on the old path. Our youth would be selfish, unreasonable, and into worldly things as are so many other young people. Our own hearts would be full of self-serving, not knowing God personally, and ready to give up on the powerless religion of self. If we hadn't followed God, we would probably be wondering now why God led us in the path of heartache untold, when it would have been our choices, not His, that led us there.

Perhaps you are like we were then—recognizing that God is bringing you to a crossroad in your life. Are fear and uncertainty holding you captive, preventing you from making a decision? Is the Holy Spirit speaking to your heart? Don't let the time for decision pass, because by not choosing to change, you have chosen to go with the worldly current.

I must be honest as I share with you. The Mary Principle can also bring confusion or heartache as we learn and try new ways. It's not always comfortable, but in the long run, it proves to be profitable for us and our children. More and more, as the years went by, I saw the value of motherhood and my precious privilege to form a child's character for Jesus.

Do you think Mary ever had to deal with confusion and heartache in raising Jesus? Of course she did! Like you and I, she had to struggle to do what was right, and she didn't always make right choices. She even lost track of her dear Son at the Passover and left for home without him. As parents, we are never going to be perfect no matter how hard we try. But when, in spite of our imperfections, we are earnestly seeking God's will, we can trust Him to supply the grace for our children to overlook our errors. And that same wonderful grace will supply what we lack in parenting skills. If we seek Him, God has entrusted these children to us as a precious treasure; we are merely partners with Him in their upbringing. He never asks something of us that He will not supply the wisdom and ability to perform.

The Mary Principle, in practical form, is found in Acts 9:6, "Lord, what wilt thou have me to do?" The Lord wants to guide us, not only with character building, but also in everything we say, do, or feel in life. In every area I used to think I could manage myself I've had to learn to say, "Lord, even though I don't feel my need of special guidance in this situation, I am choosing to seek Your will and not my own." God wants to be that personal in order to guide us, and if we will listen, we

2—P.B.T.S.

will find that He is ever sending messages to those who listen for His voice. "And they shall be all taught of God" (John 6:45).

Successful parenting is raising our children to be like Jesus. Our purpose as parents is similar to that of the grain of wheat depicted in the Bible. The tiny wheat kernel falls into the ground and supposedly dies and is buried, but in doing so it brings forth new life—a hundred times more than if it had remained alone. Parents must choose to die to self and learn to live for God. Then God's life-giving sap flows into the parent's roots first, and through them to their children. The grain of wheat puts all its effort into gathering this nourishment and life from the soil for the purpose of giving it to the next generation—its seeds. So too with parenting!

"Abide in me, and I in you. As the branch cannot bear fruit of itself, except it abide in the vine; no more can ye, except ye abide in me" (John 15:4). We must live in Jesus continually. "I am the vine, ye are the branches: He that abideth in me, and I in him, the same bringeth forth much fruit: for without me ye can do nothing" (verse 5).

The fruit represents our character, but our fruit is also our children. We need that special connection with Christ in order for His life-giving sap to flow freely through us to our children. We can pass on to the next generation only what we have obtained and possess. Through us, God can pour living springs of divine love and wisdom upon our children. As we receive His wisdom, He will enable us to nurture, admonish, and train our little ones in His way. Will you give all your life for this one purpose—connection to God?

We must be as focused and as single-minded to the task of parenting as the kernel of wheat is to producing more wheat. Does this mean that every woman must come home from the workplace to raise her children? No! Some mothers have no choice but to work outside the home. God wants to instruct *you* and teach *you* in the way *you* should go. Each of us must be free to follow God as we see Him leading us, and we must respect each other's choices. Do I think you should seriously consider staying home and raising your own children? Absolutely. But regardless of what I think, each of you must come to discern God's will for you in your present situation. Knowing God personally in our *own* experience is imperative for all of us. You, together with God, must discern His will for you!

Embracing Christ is letting God's ways take precedence over our ways. As you become more proficient in your two-way communication with God, He will reveal Himself to you in His own way, and you will grow increasingly more trusting of His guidance.

In the next chapter, I will begin sharing with you the principles that enabled me to become a tool used of God to parent my children.

THE LONE EMBRACE
A SPECIAL WORD OF ENCOURAGEMENT FOR SINGLE PARENTS

Mary, the mother of Christ, found herself an unwed mother in a society that severely punished such. It's hard for us to imagine just what obstacles she faced, knowing within her heart that she was pure but also knowing that few would believe her. Mary found out that God is very personal and that His plan for each of us is very specific. God had been waiting four thousand years for Mary to be a teenager. I believe that on the very day sin entered the human race and God promised a redeemer, He thought of Mary, knowing her all those thousands of years before and enjoying her simple faith.

In the same way God has waited for you. He has specific plans for you, and He will work on your behalf just as personally as He did for Mary. You may have been bereaved of your spouse by death, divorce, or abandonment—or you may be among the many who live with your partner, but who feel as though you might as well be a single parent because your spouse neglects parental duties. Whatever your situation, God is there for you.

Chapter 3

IT BEGINS WITH ME
"For their sakes I sanctify myself" (John 17:19).

A mother was out driving with her teenage son who had just gotten his learner's permit and was eager to drive. Her son kept "suggesting" she let him drive. Tired of his constant pestering, his mother at last gave in, but before she relinquished the wheel, she asked, "You've been watching me and know what to do, right?"

"Yeah, sure, Mom," he replied.

As he pulled out onto the road, his careful driving pleasantly surprised her. He stopped at a light, and she complimented his skills. As they head down a hill toward a busy intersection, she saw the light was going to turn red. Before she knew what was happening, her son suddenly accelerated and raced through the intersection just moments after the light changed, earning them some nasty looks, a few angry beeps, and gestures.

"Turn into that parking lot and stop!" she told him weakly. When he did so, she turned to him, still shaken. "I thought you said you'd been watching me and knew what to do."

"I have, Mom!"

"I don't think so. Let's review signals before we go on. What does red mean?"

"Stop, of course. Mom, this is silly."

"My life just flashed before me, so if you want to keep driving with me, this is not silly. Have you got that, young man?"

"Yes."

"What does green mean?"

"Go."

"And what do I do when the light turns yellow?" she asked with a meaningful look.

"You go as fast as you can to beat the light!"

You may not have had to confront your own inconsistencies quite so bluntly; nevertheless, the truth is that you can never provide for your children anything more than you have yourself. You must be honest in your self-assessment—not to become depressed and hopeless about your condition, but to prepare yourself for a radically different solution than you may have tried previously. So, if your life and religious experience is not all that you would like your children to emulate, you need to consider the changes that need to take place and let the transformation begin with you.

No one ever had a harder time of parenting than I did. And I complained to God quite a bit about the lot I faced in life. "Lord, I am so frustrated with trying to get my boys to obey! I feel that I'm warring against a gigantic obstacle that is too big for me! I can't do it!" And the pit of despair opened its arms and welcomed hopeless me. I wallowed there for awhile, rehearsing my woes. Then, as I tired of my miserable state, I found myself crying out to God again, "This is the pits, Lord! I want out!"

"Do you really want out, Sally?" the Lord asked kindly.

"Of course I really want out of my troubles! What do You mean?"

"Well, the other day you told Me you wanted out of the pit you were in, but you didn't take My hand when I extended it. I can deliver you. Did I misunderstand your request?"

I recalled the incident. I had been praying, and my heart was full of despair and hopelessness. I had tried and tried to get out of that pit myself to no avail. I visualized myself trying to climb out of the pit, but the walls were too slimy, the pit was too deep, and my strength was insufficient. I would almost make it to the top in my own strength. I could even see daylight, and then I'd loose my footing or my strength and fall back to the bottom of the pit. I'd try to think positively—and it would work for a while—but my mind always reverted to thoughts of my inadequacy and unworthiness, and I'd slip back to the bottom of that deep dark pit again.

In despair, I cried out for deliverance from Jesus. In my mind's eye, I saw God's hand extending to me. I longed to take hold of it; I wanted it more than words could express. But I didn't think I could dare believe that Jesus could deliver me. I turned my head away, feeling unworthy to take His hand. And so I remained in the pit, tortured by my ugly thoughts and feelings. Now I asked myself, "Why didn't I take God's hand?" The answer dawned: "Because I didn't feel worthy."

The Lord continued to coach my thinking and asked, *"Should you trust your feelings or My Word?"*

"Well, Your Word, of course! But my feelings tell me what I am, don't they?"

"Feelings are not to be trusted, Sally. Satan suggests his lying thoughts to your mind and then pushes your emotion buttons. Hence, wrong thoughts and wrong feelings combined exert a compelling influence to do Satan's will. He often leads you to the pit of despair in just this way, and you yield. You need not obey your feelings or the lies with which Satan taunts you. My Word can be trusted. Will you choose My Word instead of your feelings?"

Suddenly I had hope! "I don't need to listen to my feelings?" I thought. "If that's true, then I can turn away from my debilitating thoughts and emotions. I can trust Jesus! He is able and willing to save me from this pit of wrong thinking and these feelings of despair." So in my mind, I took hold of His hand, and He lifted me out of that dark, horrible pit and put my feet upon a rock—Christ Jesus!

There is no pit too deep that God's hand cannot extend to the bottom. There is no evil, no sin, too great to keep God from cleansing it or to prevent Him from taking us into His loving, forgiving, and character-transforming arms. Suddenly, I had hope.

"I don't need to listen to my feelings," I told myself. "I must go in opposition to my debilitating thoughts and emotions because they do not agree with God's Word. I can trust Jesus. He doesn't want me here."

I saw the sun breaking through the angry gray clouds of my mind. I sensed the departure of the oppressive deep darkness that had been enshrouding me. It was like Satan was losing his hold on me.

But my negative thoughts and feelings quickly returned to press me down. Again I cried out to God. "Lord, what can I do? I don't *feel* much better!"

"Don't worry about your feelings, Sally. Let's work on your thoughts. Think about the good parenting you've done. Think about the good habits you have instilled into your boys with your conscientious parenting. Come out of despair by following My leading."

It was so hard to change my thoughts. Dwelling on how awful I was and what a failure I had been was easy. It had been a life-long habit! Those same old negative thought patterns took me into the pit of despair again and again. I so longed to be free from it, I decided to put all my efforts into thinking differently than I had in the past, into finding the good, instead of the bad.

"How does this work?" I puzzled. I was really struggling to grasp the concept, and if you find yourself struggling to come out of wrong ways, believe me, it's normal. God didn't give up on me. He prompted me to recall Matthew gathering a bouquet of wild flowers, saying he loved me. God was wiping away the fog of Satan's lie that I did nothing good.

"You mean I'm not all bad? I can do good things with Jesus in me?" I asked God. Slowly, I began to realize that many of the things I had believed about myself over the years were false and that I'm worth more than gold to God. The Lord led me to actively think more positive thoughts, to build my confidence and trust in Him. "Andrew is eating less at meals because of my efforts to bring him out of overeating," I mused. "That's a good thing. And Matthew loves to go for walks with me and even work with me. Both boys love to play with me. They are learning good habits of neatness, orderliness, and thoroughness. I'm not a complete failure. I guess I do have things to rejoice about." And so my thinking, led of God, continued and changed its direction. This was a huge victory for me.

As I continued to cooperate with God, a divine peace crept into my emotions, and the ill feelings were pushed out. A light, happy spirit seemed, well, almost improper after all my years of negativity, but I cooperated with it, trusting God knew best. And joy filled the place where sorrow once reigned. "God loves me!" I thought. As I cooperated with Him, He redeemed me from the wrong thoughts and feelings that were ruling over me! I'm thankful that from that day forward, I never returned to the bottom of that pit of despair.

One of the biggest tasks we face in parenting today is to help our children overcome wrong habits of thinking, feeling, or reacting and to lead them into right habits in these areas. Without God's help, this task is impossible. Therefore, He must perform *in us* the very work we wish to see performed in our children. He must sanctify us *first*, for their sakes, and deliver us from our wrong habits of thinking, so we can, in turn, teach them what we have learned. God can, and will, impart divine wisdom and strength to every parent and child who cries out to Him for help and who cooperates with Him.

Once when Andrew was about six years old and had been very naughty, I spanked him and sent him to his room to "stop crying." After fifteen minutes, his sobs hadn't subsided at all. To distract him I sent him for a run around the house and then gave him the job of filling the wood carrier. Nothing worked! He was *still* crying. "Andrew, honey, what's the matter?" I asked. "You did your job nicely. You're not in trouble any more."

"I can't—*sniff, sniff*—stop crying," he stammered.

"Oh dear, Lord what can I do to help him? Nothing I've tried has helped."

"Sally, how did I bring you out of despair and hopelessness?" God asked, labeling the problem for me.

"Satan must be prompting him with lying thoughts," I thought. "The fact that he continues to cry shows he's cooperating with them. I need to find out what he's thinking and feeling," I said to myself, brightening at the thought.

"Andrew, what's going through your mind right now? What are you thinking?"

"How naughty and dumb I am—*boo hoo hoo*. I want to be good—*sniff, sniff*— but there must be something wrong with me because I—I can't!"

"Sally, explain to him about the pit of despair—what puts him there and what gets him out. I will be with you," the Lord encouraged me.

"Andrew, those thoughts are a lie from Satan. You don't have to obey them. It's Satan trying to push you into the pit of despair." He seemed to know just what I meant. Truly, God was with me and helped me express it just the way that would be best for Andrew to understand.

"Andrew, imagine God is reaching down His hand ready to lift you out of the pit of hopelessness. All you have to do is take hold of it. God loves you and wants to help," I smiled reassuringly. Andrew's eyes brightened. I could tell he believed me.

"Pray, Andrew, and give Jesus the bad thoughts. That's how you take his hand."

He looked at me. I nodded. And then he squeezed his eyes shut tight. "God, take my bad thoughts. Give me better thoughts. Help me be good and stop crying." He sat silently, listening for God's voice, as we've encouraged the boys to do.

The minutes ticked by. Finally, after awhile I asked, "What did God say, Andrew? What does he want you to do?"

"I think he wants me to go pick some flowers."

"Well then, that's what you better go do," I encouraged him, and off he ran.

He returned a little later with a bouquet of lilacs and *no* tears. I was so pleased for him! "What happened, Andrew?" I inquired, probing a little further.

"I asked God to take away my crying and took hold of His hand just like you said. He told me to enjoy my favorite flowers. I had to wipe away my tears so I could see and enjoy them. He cares about me, Mother. I guess I stopped crying somewhere, but I didn't notice when," he blurted out through a big toothy grin and gave me the bouquet.

Victory over self begins in our thoughts and progresses divinely to our feelings. Success came when I shared my experiences with my son. Andrew was still prone to listen to and believe the lying thoughts, but as we repeated this process, he got better and better at giving his wrong thoughts to Jesus until the victory was complete.

Our children imitate our poor problem-solving techniques. Matthew and I once saw a scene on TV of a mother throwing and breaking things in a fit of anger. Afterwards, I asked him what he had learned and he responded, "When you're mad, throw things!" What a lesson book this is for all parents! The principle is that by beholding we become changed, and that leads us to this logical question: What am I teaching by example in my home?

All too often, I realized to my shame that by my example I was teaching my boys to withdraw and enter into the same pit of despair with which I was so familiar. Thankfully only one of my boys adopted this method. This required me to revisit the same ground I had trod and teach him the same lessons God had taught me in overcoming negative thoughts, but for a time the example of my poor behavior hindered him.

I learned through this personal experience how we all need Christ to change us so that we parents can intelligently cooperate with Heaven in leading our children to Christ and gain the same experience.

I often knit when I have a few minutes. It's rewarding to reach into my bag and pull out a half-finished project and see how much I can get done in a short time. As my hands are happily creating something, I am gaining another blessing—rest. I've always been a hard worker. So when I sit down, my mind will soon start thinking about this or that thing I need to do, and I'm off to work again. I need knitting to take my mind off things, to help me sit down, rest, listen, or just relax with my family. Over the years, I have taught a number of people how to knit. I believe there are truths for us as parents even in my simple knitting basket. You can't teach knitting, for example, if you've never learned to knit. You can read books about knitting and understand the principles. You can talk about them, but without experience you can't effectively teach others to knit!

I have seen many inexperienced knitters fail at the dropped-stitch test. You see when knitting, you sometimes "drop" a stitch and don't realize it until sometime later. The experienced knitter has learned how to pick up this stitch, correct the mistake, and salvage the piece of work. Knowing about dropped stitches isn't enough. You have to master the technique of correcting the problem; you have to have practical experience. It's the same with child rearing. Any parent can *seem* to know what he or she is doing, but when a problem arises is when we see if the parent has the experience in his own life to correct the error. The problem with many of us is that we try to teach our children about God using only book knowledge or dos and don'ts; we don't have an experiential knowledge of true heart work. God encourages us to be "doers of the word, and not hearers only" (James 1:22). How can we teach our children to surrender and cooperate with God in order to be transformed and changed in heart, if we have not experienced these ourselves? Here is where many fail in parenting. We tell our children they must choose to think, say, and do the right, but we cannot teach them how to do it in Jesus because we know how only in theory.

When we experience Christ redeeming us from wrong thinking and feeling, how long is it before we can teach our children to do the same? Why, we can share the experience the very next moment! Few things will convince a child that you're genuine as watching you be transformed from a grump into a kind, patient parent who is willing to work with him. We don't need to be perfect before we share what we know, but we must have a practical experience with Christ working in us, however small it may seem at first. This is how we begin to pick up our dropped stitches in parenting.

The lesson you learn today at God's hand is a good lesson. Tomorrow's lesson will be even better. So teach what you learn today with Christ at your side. Remember, as soon as a child can love and trust his mother, he can begin to love and trust his mother's Friend Jesus.

At first, he may simply be imitating your behavior, but as the behavior is repeated, it will form a habit of trusting God, which will be instilled forever in his soul.

We have lived in the mountains of Montana for twenty years now. One of our favorite things to do is backpacking to Kintla Lake, a little-known wilderness lake nearby. We always bring a water filter with us to ensure we get pure, clean water because even here in the wilderness we can't be guaranteed that the water is not contaminated by other people or animal wastes. Jim is faithful to pump fresh water for us to drink and cook with. When the filter is placed beneath the surface, the tiny holes in the ceramic filters remove dirt, sand, floating things, disease-producing bacteria, and even *Giardia* parasites.

Spiritually, we greatly benefit if we filter our thoughts and words through Christ before we express them to our children. God must go below the surface of our words and examine our spirit and our motives, not just the outward appearance of our actions. God's Spirit will filter out all harmful, distasteful, or gritty things from our speech, emotions, and attitudes. I have found that God removes only that which is harmful. And He removes only that which we give Him permission to remove. We have a will, so our cooperation is a vital part of His cleansing and purifying process. God wants us to have happy homes with an atmosphere that will promote physical, mental, and spiritual health. But we must surrender and cooperate with His leading.

THE LONE EMBRACE
A SPECIAL WORD OF ENCOURAGEMENT FOR SINGLE PARENTS

If you feel overwhelmed at the task before you, praise God! Because it's when you feel overwhelmed that you are most likely to depend upon Him for guidance. Don't despair that your former spouse may work against your goals. Just concentrate upon the task at hand and make your home a happy place by taking Christ's hand to lead you. I once read about a man taking a cab from the airport to his hotel in a large city. The cab driver was so happy and cheerful that the man was impressed. He asked about his home and family. The cab driver's wife was dying after a long battle with cancer. The medical bills had depleted their funds until their house was in danger of foreclosure. The passenger was shocked! This cheerful man had such huge problems!

"Why, I'd expect you to be despondent," he told the driver.

"Why?" the driver responded. "It's not your fault my wife is ill. Being discouraged never helped a soul. This is my burden, and I'm thankful my problems aren't as large as those that some people have to bear."

Right now you may not feel like filtering your words and making your home happy, especially when you may have much to discourage you. But remember, you are investing for the future. You're learning that feelings don't have to control you. Happiness is contagious! So is sadness. It may not be fair that you are single, that your needs are not being met, and that you have to devote effort to parenting without a spouse to support you. However, you can depend upon God to fulfill that part of the task that you are incapable of doing.

We have been learning important lessons in preparation for parenting after Heaven's pattern—not the earthly parenting that is so commonly seen today in the homes of professed Christians. God wants His people to stand out from the normal standards of outward Christianity. He wants to distinguish your home as a Christ-led example, demonstrating an inward power to live above the pull of your flesh. He wants to do more for you and your family than you have ever imagined. And the key to unlocking Heaven's richest blessing is within your grasp, for it begins with you!

THE VOICE OF GOD

*"The Lord was not in the wind . . . not in the earthquake . . . not in the fire . . .
[but in] a still small voice" (1 Kings 19:11, 12).*

The voice of God is like the sound of many waters. There are many facets to His voice. He speaks through His Scriptures, telling us how to conduct our lives. He also speaks through nature, providence, impressions of the Holy Spirit, and our consciences. In all these, God speaks as He wills, in His timing and in His way. We need to come to understand how God speaks to our heart and soul through all these avenues.

The Bible is the backbone of all truth, and we need to test our thoughts and concepts by the Word (see Isaiah 8:20). Speaking through the Scriptures, God gives us wisdom and knowledge for the purpose of drawing us unto Himself, the Creator. In the Bible, He shows Himself as a personal God. He reveals His character so that we can recognize Him in the other voices in which He speaks. In this chapter I want to share how God speaks to us and leads us throughout the day, using avenues that are less obvious than the Scriptures but also important. God wants to walk and talk with us as He did with Enoch. Come with me.

I had just put baby Andrew in his crib, hoping he would cry himself to sleep. Despair and weariness threatened to overwhelm me. I had walked the baby most of the night, desperately trying to quiet his colic so that Jim could sleep. I had tried everything, and nothing helped. The baby was miserable, and so was I. Exhausted from many such all night vigils, I plunged into my household tasks and the care of my boundlessly enthusiastic two-year-old. All too soon I was overwhelmed, and feelings of failure crept in. "I can't do it any more!" I wailed to myself.

"What's the matter with me anyway? Why is my life so hard?" I questioned. I wondered if God was punishing me. "Lord, what a mess I am for You! I get angry and impatient. I never say the right thing at the right time. How can I go on like this? I'm just a miserable failure, Lord. Why don't You just give up on me? I used to be a good nurse, who did good things, but as a Mother, what good am I?"

Even in these early stages of despair, God was trying to speak to me, although I didn't realize it at the time. Satan had successfully diverted my mind from Christ, the source of my strength, and fastened it on my perplexities and faults. The idea of talking back and forth with God in a two-way conversation was foreign to me. But what did I have to lose? So I prayed, "Lord, I understand that I need to give You some quiet time to talk with me, and I've not knowingly done that before. I'm sure You'll want to tell me how bad I am and help me see all the things I need to change." You see, my negative ideas were coloring my perception of God!

I knelt with a heavy heart, tried my best to think of nothing, and then waited for God to straighten me out. But all that came was a tender impression—"*Sally, I love you.*"

"Oh dear!" I puzzled. "That impression must be my own thoughts, trying to tell myself things I know I don't deserve. Oh Lord, forgive me! Again, I commit myself to Your care and ask You to teach me how You will talk to me. I need Your help so much! I'm such a bad person. You have my permission to do whatever I need!" With quietness I once again awaited God's response. He impressed upon my soul, "*Sally, I love you,*" a second time, and I still doubted.

"*Sally, I love you!*" He said even more tenderly the third time.

I started to cry because somehow understanding dawned in my mind and heart that this was God speaking personally to me! How could He love dumb, failing Sally?

God knew just what to say to win my heart. The Lord was not in the wind, the earthquake, or the fire—but in a still, small voice to my mind. He saw I was headed to that prison of hopelessness and despair, and He wanted to set me free. He didn't care about my past failings. He loved me while I was yet a sinner. It at last occurred to me that everyone is unworthy. God knows this, and He is unashamed of us, no matter what we have done. Only through Him can we come out of the mess we're in.

Do you see how the voice of my flesh was striving against the voice of the Spirit? Satan pushed me to believe exaggerated views of my short-comings, while God wanted to bring me out of all those debilitating, destructive lies. The voice of God brings us challenges or new thoughts to change our perspectives and views. Being convinced He loved me is what drew me close to Him and made me ready to listen more keenly than I ever had before.

I don't know about you, but I listen better when I know I am loved. Love breaks down barriers and helps me to be willing to look differently at my thoughts. Coming out of old habits is a process, not just a one-time occurrence. This was an important beginning, and in time God got me out of my wrong thought patterns. But I had more lessons before that would become a reality.

Just as I needed to know that God loves me, our children need to know that we love them. No correction or instruction will have the desired effect if they are not secure in our love. Like Christ, we must love the sinner while we correct wrong behaviors through His power of love. I'm not speaking of an indulgent, "no-responsibility" love, but for the need of mercy and justice in the proper mix. We don't want just outward obedience from our children; we want the inward obedi-ence that springs from a willing heart and that changes their thoughts, disposition, and life.

For parents, the question is: Do we really know what our children need in correction, training, and instruction? Do they just need love and understanding? Or do they need encouragement, education, and to experience the consequences of their actions? We don't always know, do we? We often think we do, and we are often wrong. But God knows, doesn't He? Then, why don't we call upon Him? Often, we don't seek

His wisdom because we have never come to know Him as it is our privilege to know Him. So we continue in our unbalanced ways, using our human wisdom, when we could have the advice of Him who can read our child's thoughts.

The environment of love nurtures growth, and God first had to show me that He does not reject me because of my behavior, that He loves me anyway and wants to teach me how to change my wrong ways. This affected my reactions to my children. You see, if I can learn the lesson that my heavenly Father loves me—that I can call upon Him at any time and He will receive me and empower me to change—then I can train up my children in a better way, and they won't have to learn this lesson as an adult like I did. With Christ to direct our actions, we can avoid sharing the poor coping mechanisms that our parents may have unwittingly passed on to us.

The voice of God is not an audible voice. It is not a red light, flashing to indicate, "This is God, bringing this thought to your mind." His voice is a thought, a prompting, a direction, an option, or a providence from the Holy Spirit in accordance with the character and Word of God that gives a hand of direction to our present need. It operates according to Isaiah 30:21—"And thine ears shall hear a word behind thee, saying, This is the way, walk ye in it, when ye turn to the right hand, and when ye turn to the left." So we must, more than we do, judge our thoughts as to their source.

A law governs the human mind; simply stated it says: "A lie, told often enough, is finally believed." Satan, the father of lies, had used this against me, telling me again and again how unworthy I was. My feelings responded to his suggestions and had a tremendous negative influence upon me.

While Satan uses the law of a lie, Christ uses the opposite law, which is: "Ye shall know the truth, and the truth shall make you free" (John 8:32). I was slow to accept the truth that God loved me, but even so, He desired to take me deeper in this thought. One day God said, *"Sally, you are worth more than gold to Me."*

I responded, "Lord, You're too kind. I know I am worthless, but I'm so glad You still love me."

"No Sally, you are worth more than gold! Would I lie to you?"

"Well no." I still grappled with my emotions that were pushing me to repel this thought.

"Sally, I want you to say, 'I am worth more than gold.'"

"Lord, I want to obey You. I choose to obey You. But I don't believe this to be true of myself."

"I want you to say this truth out loud to Me."

God was attempting to strengthen and deepen my experience with Him by reinforcing His love and my value to Him.

"Lord . . . I'm worth . . . Oh, I can't say it; it's just not true!"

"Try again. I assure you. It is true. You can do it with Me. Believe and obey My word above your feelings."

"Ok, I'll try." I took a deep breath and said, "I'm worth . . . I'm worth . . . I'm worth more than . . . No, I just can't say it!"

"Sally, you're almost there. You can do it now."

"Oh Lord, this is so hard! What hinders me so?"

"It's just your old thought patterns, Sally. Ignore them."

Finally I said, "Lord, I'm worth more than gold—in Jesus!" Adding the "in Jesus" helped me bridge the gap. "In Jesus, I can be worthy," I thought.

"Say it once more Sally." He knew this was good for me even though I found it *very* difficult.

I said it out loud again, then again and again. And every time I said it, I gained new freedom from the lying thoughts that had ruled me so long. It got easier each time I said it, and I believed it more with every repetition. The truth, often told, finally set me free.

Does God's voice in Scripture agree with my experience? It surely does. "I will make a man more precious than fine gold; even a man than the golden wedge of Ophir" (Isaiah 13:12). God loves you and me so much that He will keep us as the apple of His eye, hide us under the shadow of His wings (see Psalm 17:8). He has graven you and me upon the palms of His hands (see Isaiah 49:16). The Bible says that I am of great value, and God confirmed it in His own sweet voice to my mind. And I finally came to believe it. "My sheep hear my voice, and I know them, and they follow me" (John 10:27).

Because of my extreme bent to the negative, I didn't need to hear how bad I was. Rather, I needed to hear how much God loved me! Our children need this same approach. They will come to an understanding of how God truly views them only when we truly display His character of love. God knows better than I just what words my child needs to hear from me to foster His love and understanding before his heart will be open to instruction and change. Through connection with Christ we can make change not only possible, but attractive. It is good for our children to face their fears and wrong habits and to discover that they can change. Human wisdom comes infinitely short of divine wisdom, hence you can see why we need to commune with God before we commune with our child—especially if a situation involves correction, because this is the area most likely to be misunderstood by our child as unloving.

This need to consult God first, before speaking to my child, even if I am sure I know what needs to be done, was God's first parenting lesson to me. Whether I was soft or firm, I had to learn to ask myself, "Am I in charge or is God? Who's leading?" And in so doing, I learned—and am still learning—how to yield to God.

How I view my relationship with God is how I will likely view my children. I wrongly believed that Christ looked upon me negatively and reproachfully, and I viewed my children in the same way. When He freed *me* from this wrong concept, He also freed *my children* because they reaped the benefit of my new understanding. I came to see that this is the foundation of all our parenting practices: We must learn to approach them as Christ approaches us.

Every parent needs to see life from God's perspective because our children will learn from us. We need to demonstrate the balance of love and firmness. God intends for our children to go higher in their experience with God than even we, their parents, have gone. It is His intention that every generation will serve Him and be restored closer to man's original condition. Unfortunately, such has not been the case. The upward process must begin somewhere, and as we discovered in our last chapter, it must begin with us. If we are going to change, *communication with God is our first step.* The more you hear His voice, the easier it becomes to recognize Him speaking amid the babble of voices competing for your attention. There is the voice of our flesh presenting its demands, the voice of Satan tempting us to sin, and the voice of God encouraging us to victory. Clearly, discrimination between these competing voices is an essential skill—and that is the focus of this chapter. Let me show you how it works in daily life through a story I've simply come to call "The Town Trip."

When we moved to Montana we didn't settle in a town or even the suburbs. No, we truly live in the wilderness. It takes an hour and a half to drive *one way* to town! A trip to town costs me at least three hours of driving time—and that's before I *do* anything. So, I quickly learned I had to be very efficient if I was to get everything done. So I plan out every store, making lists of what to get in each one.

Before I go any further, I am going to let you in on a secret about Sally Hohnberger—I like to run my own show; I'm a very organized person. So when I got in the car to go to town, I was prepared. I had a homemade lunch, the things I needed to return to stores, the things to get replacement parts for, and, of course, my list. Jim and I prayed, he kissed me goodbye, and I put the car in gear to leave, when God's still, small voice prompted me, *"Do you have your purse?"*

"Of course I have my purse," I responded.

Again the thought came, *"Are you sure you have your purse?"*

"Well, I'm sure I put it in the car." I looked, but found no purse. "Hmmm, I better see if I left it in the laundry room where I keep it."

Returning to the car with my purse in my hand, I asked, "Lord is this Your voice to me?" There was no audible voice in response, no clear impression in my mind as to yes or no. The Scriptures didn't say anything about my purse. "How can I know?" I wondered. Yet I sensed it *was* God speaking to me. I'm so thankful I didn't leave without my list and purse. My trip would have been wasted without them.

"If God cares enough about me to save me from forgetting my purse and all the consequences that misfortune would bring," I told myself, "He must care about all the little things in my life!" Coming to a decision, I prayed, "Lord, You have my permission to interrupt my thoughts at any time today, because I know You are my best Friend. Help me recognize Your voice." He is always there for us.

Those thoughts led me back to our days in Wisconsin when I first began to understand God's love and watchcare and started to see His loving, guiding hand in my life. I had decided to go to Him about Andrew's colic because, frankly, I was at the end of my rope after five months. I was nursing, not bottle feeding, so what could be the problem? As I prayerfully considered my situation, an idea came into my thoughts. "Adjust your diet," it seemed to say. This was a totally new concept for me, and I knew God must be trying to tell me something. Maybe I was eating something that was contributing to Andrew's colic. Acting on this new thought, I read different books. I talked to anyone who would listen to my story. I prayed. As a result, I decided to remove all stimulating foods and spices from my diet. But Andrew's colic still did not improve.

The voice of Scripture doesn't speak to the specific issue of colic, so I couldn't look for the answer there. But I did seek God's help through prayer, hoping He would impress me with another thought. I got no answer. Yet I trusted He would show me somehow.

Providence is another voice of God. Nothing happens in our lives without the approval of an all-knowing God. What some call fate or coincidence is all too often the working of a providential God. Therefore, I know it was God who led me to a certain dietitian who suggested that meat can be a stimulant, too, and that I should try eliminating it from my diet for a while and see what happened with Andrew. After I ate vegetarian for two days, Andrew's colic was gone! It had worked, and I was filled with gratitude to my Friend who loved me and helped me. For the first time, Andrew slept for five hours straight—a record! He became a sweet, happy, and contented baby. With increased sleep, my disposition became happier and more positive. God was becoming a real Friend. No, it wasn't an overnight transformation into full, continuous communion with God. For me, the process was little by little, but there were definite changes. God longs to direct us out of our troubles. My prayers were becoming more personal, my trust greater. Timidity and insecurity still exerted their influence, but God never gave up on me as I grew and developed confidence in Him. I had no idea how soon I would need that trust and confidence.

One day I left two-year-old Matthew playing in the sandbox with Shilo, our Brittany Spaniel, while I went upstairs to put Andrew down for his nap. I paused for just a moment, delighted to see him happily settle in for sleep without his little body stiffened in pain from the colic. I returned downstairs and discovered Matthew was no longer in the sandbox! Where had he gone? I looked out each window, checking all the usual spots my adventurous son would typically be. He was not to be found. I ran outside, calling him, but there was no answer! I tried calling Shilo. The dog didn't respond either, and the beginnings of panic set in.

I quickly found Jim, and together we systematically began searching the forty acres of our property, most of which was wooded and filled with underbrush. Terrible thoughts raced through our minds. Local farm dogs had been known to form a pack and had taken down deer. Would they attack a little child? Instinctively, I ran into the woods following various paths. After a while, I came to a clearing near our pond. Oh no, could he have fallen into the water and drowned? Now I really worried. Matthew loved playing in the water and had no fear of it, although he couldn't swim. I ran the shoreline looking for any trace of him, but found nothing. Jim, too, was running, and searching. I could hear him calling Matthew. Almost frantic, we met in a field. "Let's pray!" Jim suggested, and we did. "God, You know where Matthew is. At two years old, he talks very little, but his physical coordination excels. That's not good. Help us find him!"

No impressions were distinguishable amid the fearful emotions flooding our souls. Logic demanded a different plan. Jim suggested we call all our neighbors to help us make a systematic search. But while Jim was on the phone, I couldn't rest.

"Lord, where should I look? I need to be calm. Give me the calmness and logic I need for this situation. I know You will guide me to where I need to go—somehow." I looked at the possible directions Matthew might have gone and decided that a little boy might wander off into the woods behind the sandbox. God leads our logic and reason when we ask Him to. As I started down the path, I realized I had been there twice already and that Jim had searched there as well without success. Yet I sensed this is where I should be. "Matthew? Shilo?" I called. Matthew might be lost, but Shilo wasn't likely to be. I kept calling for Shilo. Finally, he came running.

"Where is Matthew, Shilo?" I demanded. He began to run up the path in the direction from which he had come. I followed until he stopped at a fork. I was hoping for a "Lassie" experience. Shilo hesitated; his leading became indistinct and uncertain.

"Lord, which way now?" I *sensed* I should turn right. I followed this path with Shilo at my heels. "And thine ears shall hear a word behind thee, saying, This is the way, walk ye in it, when ye turn to the right hand, and when ye turn to the left" (Isaiah 30:21). I was living this verse, although I didn't know it at the time. Entering a clearing, I called Matthew once more, listening intently for any sound. I thought I heard something to my left. "This way, Lord?"

I *sensed* the answer was yes, and I walked through a clearing into another wooded area. And there was Matthew just ahead of me, about twenty feet away! He was sitting on the ground, hung up on a short piece of barbed wire fence that was snagged by a tree branch that was stuck just sufficiently to keep it in place.

How does God lead us directly to the place we need to be when we don't really understand His leading? I don't know. God is God and can do these things, even if we can't explain how He does it. Truly He loves and communicates with us. How did He manage to time a sound from Matthew to my listening? He is awesome! God used impressions, my senses, my reason, and His providential leading. All were His voice to guide my steps.

Unspeakable joy seized me as I released Matthew from his barbed-wire bondage and scooped him up. Surprisingly, he was perfectly at peace and had enjoyed his adventure, completely unaware of any danger. Running back into our yard, I saw the neighbors' cars as these dear people had dropped everything to come to our aid. Even as I neared them, I heard Jim giving instruction on the system to use to search the woods. "He's found! The lost is found!" I shouted over and over. And celebration reigned where anxiety had ruled but moments before.

Our God is just that personal! He can even lead us to our missing child. And in the day-to-day business of life, He wants so much to communicate with us to help us in the management of our children. Do we call upon Him? Do we take the time to talk with Him, to seek His counsel and then to listen for His voice? Do we know His voice? Our part is to cry out to Him in our need, to listen, and to choose to cooperate with His ways. It takes some study to learn Christ's character and some experimentation to recognize the voice of God. He can't do the listening or studying for us, but if we will put forth the effort, we will find it well worth the work.

God's part is to hear our cry, to inspire our course of action, and to give us right thoughts to think. Then, when we cooperate, His divine power pours into our life, subduing our fearful thoughts, emotions, and feelings—in His timing, in His way. God will do all that we cannot do. Satan and all the hosts of hell cannot defeat the weakest human thus connected to God. We cannot do God's part—saving and empowering us—but oh, how many sincere people try and fail as they attempt to save themselves, for it is beyond human power. Humanism is trying to do God's will in our own power. And when we do this, we pay homage to a powerless god.

As we learn how to recognize God's voice and cooperate with Him to change our disposition and character, this living *example* demonstrates to our children how they, too, can be led by and empowered of God. Children learn mostly *by our example*, good or bad. They will become what we put before their eyes for them to imitate. If God is ever to lead us in the management of our children, we need to become God's children. We need to learn to recognize His voice and gain the experience of heeding that voice. As we learn these basics, led by Christ, we will have a testimony to share with our children that will bring real wisdom and power to our parenting. Parenting shouldn't just become behavior modification in the power of the flesh, but rather character development and practical training in the power of Jesus Christ, our Savior and Creator.

How can we be sure it is the voice of God impressing our minds? How can we avoid being deceived?

All the voices of God—be they found in the Bible, His providence, impressions of the Holy Spirit, reason, conscience, nature, or a friend's counsel—will agree when God is leading. Satan's voice brings confusion and conflicting voices. When in doubt, ask yourself a few simple questions: Does the voice, thought, or emotion agree with the revealed Word of God? If it does, it will promote trust rather than fear, love rather than hate, patience and kindness rather than harshness or anger. Does the voice or thought promote actions in line with the principles of God's kingdom? Does the thought come in the spirit of God, offering His helping hand, or in Satan's spirit of compulsion and force?

Scripture can be safely regarded as authoritative in all matters to which it speaks. However, many situations are not clearly addressed in the Bible. If the Scriptures don't directly confirm or deny the thought or impression in question, look at the underlying principle.

One day, after moving to the mountains, I was out on the back porch resting and taking in the beauties of nature surrounding me. As I sat there, quiet and thoughtful, a simple impression drifted into my thoughts. *"Sally, you need to talk with Jim about* ———*,"* and God named a specific view Jim held incorrectly.

"Oh no, Lord! Jim's got a temper. I can't do that! Tell Jim he is wrong? This must be the devil talking to me. But what if this is You, Lord? Is it?"

Again a quiet, little voice said, *"Sally, you need to talk with Jim about this."*

"Lord, You know how much my personality hates conflict. But I'm willing to do this if it's You speaking to me."

"Yes Sally, I will be with you. Take My hand, and we will do this thing together. Trust Me!"

I looked at the grass, the trees, and the lofty summits of the mountain peaks reaching up to heaven. I followed nature's voice by reaching my hand into the air as if to take Jesus' hand into mine.

I walked into the living room where Jim was working at the desk and said, "Jim, would you like to go for a walk with me now? I know you're busy. It's all right, if you can't." Secretly I was hoping he wouldn't want to go for a walk. I knew his personality well, and it was highly unlikely he would agree to go. After all, once Jim is immersed in a task, he doesn't like to break from it.

"Oh sure, honey," he responded, "I'd love to go for a walk with you. I'm free right now!" And he enthusiastically put all his papers aside.

"Oh dear!" I said to myself, "Now I'm stuck." The voice of providence just confirmed the impression that God's voice and nature had taught. I sensed strongly now that this prompting was of the Lord. "Lord, I'm trusting Your strength and not my weakness." We had barely begun our walk, and before I lost my nerve, I quickly told Jim what God had put on my heart.

"Sally, where did you get that silly idea?" Jim asked—and began defending himself.

In the past, I tried to solve problems by minimizing conflict. If anyone strongly disagreed with my comments, I'd back down even if I felt I was right. Under the stress of conflict, my mind became like a paper shredder. I couldn't put two thoughts together in any sort of logical argument. Now, as Jim disagreed with me, I felt myself beginning to let go of my thoughts as I had always done in these situations.

"Sally, don't let go! You don't have to let go! I'm here with you; trust Me! This is not a good way to respond to difficulties. I have a better way. Trust Me! You can do fine in Me!"

I imagined taking Jesus' hand again right there on the road while Jim was talking. For the first time, I was able, through the power of Christ, to continue the conversation with Jim to its completion without losing control of my thoughts. It was a miracle I had never dreamed possible! We talked throughout that twenty-minute walk, and in the end, although Jim and I didn't agree, we went back into our day without a wall between us. I didn't feel that same load of guilt and upheaval I usually felt after conflict. In the past, I might have withdrawn and not talked to Jim the remainder of that day, but instead my heart was drawn out toward him. This time I didn't need to distance myself from him.

The next morning Jim told me that God revealed to him in his prayer time that I was right, and he thanked me for bringing the subject up to him. Wow! Out of such experiences, my confidence in the voice of God grew. And in just such ways, God wants you to step into the school of Christ too, where He will teach you to know His voice by experience.

When God asked me to talk with Jim, I wasn't sure it was His voice. Testing the impression through providence reassured me it was, but it was still a judgment call. After the experience, I was *very* sure it was of God because of the fruit.

When we stop to evaluate our experiences, it is usually quite clear whether it was God speaking to us or not. Sometimes we'll make mistakes and errors in judgment. But we can learn from both positive and negative outcomes. Thankfully God is not waiting to zap us if we make mistakes. He wants us to learn how we can do better next time.

Impressions of the Holy Spirit are another key avenue that God uses to communicate with you and me. But we should never assume that every thought is from God. We should test impressions by the Scripture, providential leadings, reason, and conscience to confirm what appears to be God's voice. John says, "Believe not every spirit, but try the spirits whether they are of God: because many false prophets are gone out into the world" (1 John 4:1). Satan can use even Scripture to lead us astray, so close discernment is vital. When Satan tempted Jesus in the wilderness, he quoted true Scripture to Him, but he did so in a spirit of mistrust, and that spirit is uniquely Satan's character.

If the voice is of God, it will give perfect liberty. God wants willing obedience. This is of greater value to Him than just outward conformity or begrudging service. God's suggestions give us full freedom to choose for or against Him. If we choose against Him, He still pursues us with love and tenderness.

But choosing against Him carries consequences. He allows these consequences to come in love, to awaken us to our need of Him and to bring about change in our lives. Christ is ever pursuing us. He gives us time to reason and decide. There is no compelling or force in the Spirit of Christ.

The spirit of Satan operates differently. He may begin by giving you his thoughts as a suggestion, but if you choose against him, his spirit resorts to compulsion and force. Satan is like a high-pressure salesman who tells you that you must decide this moment, that tomorrow your golden opportunity will be gone. Satan pushes you to hasty decisions. Bringing you under his influence, he doesn't give you time to think. If you hesitate at all, he fears you will say no to him or see his devices, so he pushes the buttons of your wrong emotions. These emotions compel you to use your poor problem-solving techniques which keeps you under his control. From that day to this, I have never returned to letting go of my thoughts and being incapacitated.

We need to use care that we don't resort to the same spirit Satan uses in our interaction with our children. We have been exposed to Satan's spirit of force our whole lives, and it's not surprising that we tend to adopt it as our own. Even if we are a hundred percent right in what we are asking our children to do, if our spirit is like Satan's, we are one hundred percent wrong in our approach and cannot accomplish any real good. The truth without the Spirit of God is a curse, not a blessing. Therefore, if we speak the truth to our child in correction, but have a wrong spirit full of harshness and anger, we work against the very things we desire.

No matter how many things we have done wrong in our parenting, we don't have to obey Satan's lying, deceptive thoughts or compelling emotions any longer. Jesus will free us from this bondage when we call upon Him and follow Him. God longs to speak with us through His Word, His Holy Spirit, providential leadings, nature, impressions, conscience, and reason to lead us in the path of victory. "My sheep hear my voice, and I know them, and they follow me" (John 10:27).

THE LONE EMBRACE
A SPECIAL WORD OF ENCOURAGEMENT FOR SINGLE PARENTS

So many examples in this chapter are near and dear to my heart because they remind me how much God loves me and how He communicates with me. All these experiences led me to God for the specific solutions I needed. Each of these trials found me responding more and more to Christ. Each one strengthened my hold on Him. He always answered me, not always in my desired timing, but always in the timing

He knew was best. If God cares about such minor things, is he not interested in your larger struggles—money, time, the never-ending conflicts of work and child care? Is He not also interested in the extraordinary interpersonal relationships your situation has left you with, not only dealing with a former spouse in many cases, but often with the stresses of forming and maintaining a blended family? Know with certainty that Jesus understands and cares and welcomes you with open arms, no matter how discouraged you may feel. Go to Him. Learn how to distinguish His voice to your mind and soul, for it is vitally essential. We all need this fellowship with Christ continually. We can't get along without it!

Chapter 5

GOING UP TO THE MOUNTAIN

"And Moses went up unto God, and the Lord called unto him out of the mountain, saying, Thus shalt thou . . . tell the children" (Exodus 19:3).

Before moving to Montana I had only rarely been exposed to real mountains. After all, I grew up in the Midwest, hardly an area renowned for its mountain ranges. Now, living in the Rocky Mountains, I have learned to love their rugged grandeur, but I have also learned it takes real effort to climb a mountain. I've climbed many. Your muscles ache; your legs get weary and cry out to stop; your breath comes in ragged gulps, and as you negotiate dangerous sections, you soon learn that there are situations and activities for which no antiperspirant made is sufficient. Getting to the summit of the mountain is a thrill worthy of our effort.

Now if I find all this activity to be hard work, imagine what it was for Moses when God called him up Mount Sinai. Moses was eighty years old at the time, and I can see him in my mind's eye putting forth the effort to climb that mountain with its steep and rugged paths to *draw near to God.* Moses had been called to something, and he went forth with joy and great anticipation when he was called. He delighted in communion with His Maker. He didn't claim his age as an excuse, nor did he seek more clarification before obeying. He didn't stand at the foot of the mountain and yell, "What?" He knew that splendor and affirmation awaited him. You and I have an invitation, too—no, more than an invitation. We have a command to go up the mountain and meet with God.

If my love, my Jim, my Prince Charming, were at the top of the mountain, I'd climb that mountain with bursting love in order to get there, just to be with him. Neither grizzly bears nor fallen trees could keep me from going to the summit to be with him. Like Moses, I'd climb over steep precipices and face any arduousness with joy—all for the blessed opportunity of spending time with my love. Going up the mountain to have time with God should be that rewarding.

I compare Moses' going up the mountain to our learning the art of a two-way conversation with our Lord in our *personal worship time.* It's often arduous. Why? One time God speaks so sweetly and gives us a solution right away. Then another time He seems so silent and far away. It tries our patience to learn the lesson of waiting on God to speak or not to speak—and finding peace either way.

Being consistent in our time with God also takes exertion, much like climbing a mountain. But it's worth it to gain an audience with the King of kings! Moses learned how to talk with God as with a friend. He learned the art of simply telling God his problems and listening quietly for God's response. So must we.

Moses was the leader of his people, and we parents are the leaders of our families. As parents, we must successfully overcome the obstacles we face in maintaining a two-way conversation with God before we can safely lead our children over the obstacles they face in coming to know God. Communion with God is how we find solutions to our problems. We may not have a literal mountain to climb, as did Moses, yet every one of us is called up to the mountain to have our *personal time* with God.

Most of us sincerely desire a close, personal relationship with God. Yet somehow it eludes us. In this chapter, I'd like to explore with you how you can, if you are willing, transform your personal worship time from a period of study, or even of prayer, to a special daily time communing with God, deeply, intimately, as did Moses—different, and more empowering, than anything you have experienced before. Through the Holy Spirit, God wants to commune with you as with a friend to interpret the Scriptures to meet your needs and understanding this very day. This *intimate communication* is the key, not only to that close personal walk with God we desire, but to overcoming every obstacle we face as a parent. So how do we experience this? Come, climb the mountain with me.

When I read my Bible or any good literature, I ask God to direct my mind to interpret it correctly. In this way, I assume the position of a student before the great Teacher. After reading a small portion or a verse, I sit back to contemplate with God what I've read. He draws near and gives me thoughts and applications that are so simple, yet profound and life-changing in their application in Him. God imparts His wisdom to us in this way. He doesn't speak in an audible voice, but brings thoughts to our minds in order to direct our steps (see Isaiah 30:21).

Climbing can be just plain arduous at times. Consistently putting one foot in front of the other requires exertion and self-discipline. Fatigue and the unfamiliarity of the task can invite distraction. Satan knows this and does everything he can to oppose our efforts to come to God. He tries to control circumstances to crowd out our quiet time with God. He successfully uses the obstacles of distraction or inconsistency to keep us from trying to connect with God and taking time to hear His solutions to our problems. Climbing over these obstacles on the mountain is hard, but it's worth the effort. Few of us realize just how personal God desires to make our instruction. He knows just what is before us this day, and He wants to prepare us by connecting us to His wisdom.

What do these obstacles look like, practically?

"Lord I seem to meet so many obstacles when I come to You in the morning. I long to draw near to You as Moses did, but it seems I'm opposed on every side. For example when I creep out of bed in the morning, tiptoe very quietly down the stairs, and silently open my Bible—my child will often wake up with a *Wanhhh!*, demanding my attention and crowding out my time to seek and connect with You. Why is that?"

"Sally you are not warring against flesh and blood but against powers, principalities, and rulers of darkness. Satan is constantly opposing your climb up the mountain to Me. He pushes the negative emotional buttons in your child or you in order to keep you from connecting with Me.

3—P.B.T.S.

"Remember climbing those steep precipices on your last mountain climb? You had to stretch your legs beyond your comfort zone, and you couldn't pull up that long stretch until Jim, who was above you, took your hand for a boost up. Likewise, you need to grasp My hand to get over these hurdles. I'll teach you in the way you should go in handling your emotions of frustration and your child's upset feelings. I'm here to teach you."

"Lord that gives me courage to try again—and I will. I also have the obstacle of inconsistency that hampers my coming to you in the morning. I have good intentions, but circumstances keep me from You. I get to bed late the night before, so getting up is hard. The phone rings during my quiet time, stealing my time with Jesus. The furnace makes noises that demand attention, and my mind wanders to my shopping list. So what do I do with these distractions?"

"Separated from Me, you will lack wisdom, courage, and strength. This is why Satan is so persistent to distract you. Circumstances are not to rule you. You must learn to rule over your circumstances using Heavenly wisdom. Seek Me first before you respond to the distractions in order to filter what should and what should not be done. I will help you! Some distractions will still come. I let some come to you to train you in a better way of responding to them by coming to Me first. Many things can be deferred for later. I'll instruct you, if you come to Me."

Whatever the obstacles that keep you from climbing the mountain to God in the morning, He has a solution for you. Time with God, gaining His perspective and solutions, will resolve every difficulty or distraction. Taking His hand will get us over every obstacle that is too large for us. He loves to have us call upon Him. Every soul can find the strong hand of Jesus stretched out to clasp their hand. Put your trust in the Lord and climb your mountain to Him to connect to His wisdom and strength.

As Moses went up the mountain to learn from God the divine instructions for the Israelites, we climb our mountain to pray and commune with God in the morning, giving Him the opportunity to share His directions for us today so that, in turn, we can tell our children what God has said. Sometimes that will be carried out in morning or evening family worship in a general way. Other times that will be shared between husband and wife, deciding on a course together for the family. Maybe there will be the need of a family counsel, deciding as a family the action to be taken. Most commonly, this communication will take the form of a private conference between parent and child with specific counsel. This teaching can be in the form of encouragement, instruction, reproof, a call to change, consequences for disobedience, a plan for change, or simply a call to a decision. If we learn to go to the mountain and get our instruction from God, then, as parents, we can be effective tools in Jesus' hand. For most of us this is going to mean on-the-job training. Let me share one incident.

Andrew was silent and stubborn. I have to admit that I didn't feel too cheery either. We had just had a typical conflict over sweeping the floor. I wasn't sure where to go next, but the Lord knew. *"Sally, how is your spirit?"* He asked tenderly.

"Well, to be honest, Lord, I'm ready to give him what he deserves right now and *make him* sweep that floor the right way. He knows better, and he needs to start exercising some self-government!"

"But Sally, isn't your spirit the same stubborn spirit you see in your son right now? Come apart and let's talk things over," the Lord encouraged me.

Part of me wanted to, and part of me didn't. With just that moment of interruption from God, I could see both sides more clearly now. I decided I didn't want to resort to anger and force to get Andrew to obey. "God's way is better. I'll try God" I thought and excused myself for some time alone in the bathroom with God.

"Lord, what shall I do with Andrew?" I asked. There was silence for thirty seconds, then sixty seconds. It seemed endless. "I need to get out there so that breakfast can be ready on time." Slowly, my true need surfaced in the quiet. "Oh Lord, I'm not happy nor at peace. I need to get rid of all these pushy emotions in myself. Please take all this yuk I have in my heart right now."

I relaxed and let it all go. "This too, can be a little thing." I decided. "I know You'll help me work it through." I prayed and asked God to be my King. I was willing, now, to be His subject. Making sure our hearts and spirits are sweet is always the first step in any child rearing conflict. And God did show me how to bring Andrew around the "right" way, and because my spirit was sweet, he responded in like manner.

God created us for fellowship with Him; He waits for you and me early in the morning so that we can have time to talk together. When we don't come, God is disappointed (see Jeremiah 29:19). He will be there tomorrow waiting, because He loves us.

However, there is a heart work that needs to be done in coming before the Lord. That work involves giving up my will and receiving God's will in its place. Heart work is a lot of letting go of self and a lot of allowing Christ to work in me that which He desires. This is hard to do because we are not naturally inclined to welcome any change that denies us our desires. Choosing to submit to God's will is what the Bible speaks of as having the mind of Christ—and learn it we must. We must give God the Pilot's position in every thought, feeling, and response in our lives. And I must assume the co-pilot's position of listening and cooperating as He leads.

This heart work is much like housekeeping. Like our homes, our hearts also require cleansing, sorting, and ordering of our thoughts, feelings, inclinations, habits, motives, and desires. Jesus is a gentle Savior; He never works faster than we are able to bear. When we are willing to let our self-will be swallowed up, He can raise us up in newness of life, and we can go forth into the day vitalized with His right thoughts, feelings, and hope! This is God's desire for the end product of our private time together on the mountain.

When God called Moses up into the mountain, the people were to prepare themselves for two days to come before the Lord and receive His commandments. So, too, we must make certain preparations before coming to the Lord. Tomorrow's choice to connect with the Savior begins with the time I choose to go to bed. Is it early enough that I can have the expectation of rising in the morning and climbing that mountain before my duties as a parent crowd out and overwhelm my desires for God?

At first, even with an earlier bedtime, it was a difficult series of choices for me. I mean to stop hugging my pillow, crawl out of bed, and go downstairs. But my legs don't want to move; they cry out for me to return to my warm bed. I learned not to heed their protests. God's still, small voice spoke to my heart, personally calling me to worship. By getting up, I yielded to the call of the Spirit. I sensed God's presence with me—not physically, but in my soul. I sensed how pleased He was that I came to have fellowship with Him. A song based on Scripture entered into my head, and I sang, "Humble yourself in the sight of the Lord . . . and He shall lift you up" (see James 4:10). I knelt reverently to pray, and you know what? When I lingered in God's presence, He spoke personally to me, giving advice on the real needs in my heart and in my work of parenting. No matter how baffled or discouraged I have felt, I have found the Scriptures to be true and that God has lifted me up. For the last twenty years, I have studied child rearing as my primary study and have discovered that the study of child rearing is really learning how I am to be a child to God. I've found it exhaustless, meaningful, and rewarding.

When Moses climbed up the mountain, he waited before the Lord for *six days* before God called him into His presence to talk! I don't know about you, but I find God's silence feels too long when I wait for six *minutes!* I've often wondered if I would have the patience to endure such a test of waiting. Where do we gain this patience? In *waiting!*

God wants no divided service. To be focused on God, Moses had to set aside his daily cares—and with hundreds of thousands of people depending upon him, Moses certainly had lots of cares and worries. The human mind easily wanders. We've all had it happen to us. I remember praying, when all at once an item for my shopping list just popped into my head and diverted my thoughts. Another time, it was a family difficulty that just had to be resolved *my* way. Things like this draw us from God even in our special time to connect with Him.

So how do we deal with these distractions?

First, realize that you are *training* your mind to exercise a new skill and that your lack of focus doesn't mean a lack of desire—just the need for training. Second, when you recognize that your mind has wandered away, just bring it back. Emptying the mind of clutter and distractive things is truly a discipline—because it requires a decision to turn away from them as often as they arise and to remain focused where God wants you.

Letting God lead us is a necessity; waiting grows patience, a contented Spirit, and trust in God (see James 1:4). Yet how many of us come before God without any preparation, without any self-evaluation? We give God our shopping-list prayer of what we want Him to do for us today. God is not to be our errand boy, but rather our Ruler, our Lord, and our King. The position of king and ruler is one that we have wrongly occupied. We must consciously relinquish it and allow God to take His rightful place in the relationship. Time with God is for getting to know Him personally through communion. It's honest self-evaluation time; it's making plans with God to change me; it's forging a vital connection with God that empowers me to change; and it's putting God in the position of Lord to lead me through every difficulty in my day. These are the most important purposes for this time.

I recall when I first realized I was being granted an audience before the throne of grace. We were driving thirty hours from Montana to Wisconsin to visit our family, and it was my turn at the wheel. It was one o'clock in the morning, so I thought how nice it would be to spend this time talking with God while my family slept. I started praying, but in the midst of my talk with the Lord, I did something I might have done with a friend, but had never considered doing with God. The casual setting just seemed to encourage free-flowing conversation, and I asked God, "How are so and so doing?"

I really wasn't expecting an answer, but my mind was tuned heavenward, and God responded, *They aren't doing so well.*"

"Lord, please sustain them." I said. "Give them wisdom by Your power and grace. What are they struggling with?" And He told me just what was going on.

At this moment, I recognized I truly had an audience before the King of kings. I listened more intently; this was my golden opportunity! I began to search my mind earnestly for every question I could think of that had troubled or concerned me, and He answered every one as He saw fit. It was over an hour later when I ran out of questions. Then I prayed, "God, inspire me with any further questions I should ask of You."

And He did.

I was disappointed when my questions ended. This must be a taste of what Moses experienced. After two hours, Jim awoke to ask me how I was doing driving. I had been so attentive and tuned into God that I was able to tell Jim almost every detail. We later found all I was told to be true. God desires to be just this personal with all of us, if we will speak to Him as a friend and make opportunities for communication.

One of my favorite places to gain this "mountaintop" experience was soaking in a warm tub in the evening while Jim was watching the boys. Busy mothers don't get much quiet time to think or reflect, and this became my special time with God. I referred to it as my "baptismal tub bath." I would evaluate and review my day's responses and be willing to die to self here. I learned to let God touch the sensitive areas of my inner character flaws and found He was truly there to help me to change. After dealing with my personal character defects, I was prepared to pour out my heart's burdens about my children. And, in turn, God often gave me special ideas and insights into changing the weak character traits in my sons through His wisdom and direction. It was marvelous, and it worked! I felt as though I had a General helping me work out a battle plan and that I could not fail. When I exercised this faith in Christ, it moved the mountain of self—not only in me, but also my children. I always returned to my family from this "mountaintop tub" experience as a mother renewed! I think this was how Jesus must have felt—recharged for a new day after communing with His Father while here on earth.

This special time with God wasn't just for my evening soak in the tub. In the morning, God also helped me plan for my day. With God, I would even decide what household duties were needful, which ones I should omit, and what corrective procedures I should incorporate with my children. I'm inclined to overwork, so God and I had to plan in some fun to help me find a balance. All this came out of my quiet time alone with God at the beginning of the day.

Planning is good, but the real good is found in developing balance in my day-to-day life. I've learned to balance the time I spend with my child developing skillful work habits, schooling, and character training with some time spent in having fun together. I've learned not to be dogmatic and box myself into a corner with my zeal to correct and reprove. So I defer correction for later. In my eagerness to do everything God has shown me, I've sometimes forgotten to take Jesus with me so that I remain sensitive to my child's feelings and need for balance. So to make sure I filter my thoughts and words through Christ, I'd often have to withdraw from the scene. I've found that five or ten minutes walking down the road, talking and reconnecting with God, brings divine peace and a good direction to my heart, which enables me to properly and effectively approach my child in profitable correction in Christ. Going up to the mountain to gain the right Spirit through Christ allows me to offer that same Spirit and personal God to my child.

Moses went up to the mountain to spend time with God, and he returned with renewed energy and wisdom to take up his duties of leading the children of Israel. God made a covenant that He would be their God, and they would be His people. God freed them from slavery and promised to bring them to Canaan. So, too, with us today. God has promised that if we will hear and obey His voice, He will bless abundantly and bring us into the Promised Land. My heart can be at peace, and my children can learn to obey in Him. Every parent is called up to the mountain to receive instruction—one-on-one instruction from God on how to nurture and train up our children in the ways of God.

Child care is perhaps the most demanding job in the world. Moses gained something from his time on the mountain. *He gained God's perspective.* He saw the overwhelming problems he faced in caring for his "family" as God sees them—minor and easy to manage. Today, we become discouraged and frustrated, too, when we look at the problems in raising our families. We need the perspective that Moses gained on the mountain. We need to understand what God can and will do for us.

Join me on a day when a typical problem had a most unusual solution.

"It's your fault!"

"No, it's not! It's yours, and I'm going to tell Mother!"

I heard them coming. How could I *not* hear! "Oh Lord," I prayed, "I am so weary of these conflicts with my boys—arguing with each other, each blaming the other, and no one admitting they're wrong. What shall I do with them?"

"Maybe Jim could help you?" God's still, small voice directed me. So I called a halt to the noise and went to find Jim.

"Honey, I'm so frustrated. I need to go outside for a walk to get peace. Will you take care of the boys until I get back? They've been arguing again. I need a new approach."

"Sure, I'll watch them," Jim agreed.

I went outside to give God my wrong thoughts and emotions. In the meantime, Jim took the boys aside to settle their disagreement. Jim called out to God for help and in this process discovered a great solution.

"Okay boys, that's enough explanation for me! I don't know who did what, but you both know the truth. I want you to settle your own dispute here. Matthew, you go to the front porch and ask God what *you* should do to solve this problem. Andrew, you go to the back porch and ask God what He'd have *you* do to solve this problem. Then I want the two of you to get together and resolve this yourselves."

I returned while the boys were still on the porches. All my emotions were at peace, but I had no ideas or solutions for the situation. Jim explained what had happened while I was away, and I decided to keep still and watch the outcome. When both boys were ready, they discussed the situation with calm attitudes and worked out an agreeable resolution. Each boy made some concessions to his brother's view, and each apologized for where he was wrong.

We all would do well to go up this mountain to God!

God needs to be a part of any resolution for disputes. Faith believes God is able to handle the problems we face and trusts in Him—not in a methodology of a specific consequence for a specific infraction. Too many parents trust in a methodology and know not God. Many parents ask me, "When my child does this, what should I do?" waiting for me to prescribe a specific course of action as if that is the secret to success. When I tell them about going up the mountain to find out what God wants them to do, they become honestly and sincerely baffled. They listen and nod their heads, but they turn aside from Him who reads their child's thoughts and ask me, "Now, how do I get them to eat their peas?"

We must change from serving this powerless god of *our* own wisdom and learn to trust in God's leading. I'm not opposed to specific information. However, a process that works today isn't guaranteed to work the same tomorrow. It all depends upon where the child's heart is. God alone knows the end from the beginning, so the secret to gaining our child's heart is to consult with Him for guidance.

When dealing with the rebellious minds of Korah, Dathan, and Abiram, Moses needed wisdom to judge in the moment of crisis and conflict. What did he do? He turned to God for the answer. Did God know what was right to do? Yes. God first used the mild measure of reason and then gave time for repentance. When the rebels chose independence from God and yielded to the spirit of treachery, then God, judging their hearts rightly, turned to a severe consequence—opening up the earth to swallow them.

Later, we see God use a different methodology in a similar conflict with Miriam and Aaron. Miriam coveted Moses' position of authority just as Korah had done and was reprimanding Moses wrongfully. This time God didn't use mild measures first. He immediately imposed leprosy on Miriam as a consequence for her envy and jealousy. Moses pled with God to heal her and forgive her. God knew that although she and Aaron were erring, their hearts were still tender and willing to be corrected. He knew Moses would respond in love to their rebellion for He had put this in Moses' heart. It was Moses' example that touched Miriam's heart so effectively and brought this dispute to a good end. We, too, must turn to God for direction in the moment!

Are we, through God's grace and power, living what we are asking our children to do? God can heal our blindness, deafness, and paralyzed condition. Our largest influence upon our children is our example, and it affects them far more than words. Often our actions speak so loudly that our children cannot hear our words. Many youth tell me hypocrisy lives in their homes, and thus they give up on God, the faith they were raised in, and the church, thinking it's all a farce. Religion is powerless if it doesn't change *me*!

To follow the example of Moses, to go up the mountain, to commune with God is a blessed, wonderful experience, and it awaits all who are willing to put forth the effort to obtain it. As you and I come to learn the voice of God to our soul, we will make fewer and fewer mistakes and develop confidence in God's leading. So have faith that Jesus will teach you as He did Moses. "As I was with Moses, so I will be with thee" (Joshua 1:5).

THE LONE EMBRACE
A SPECIAL WORD OF ENCOURAGEMENT FOR SINGLE PARENTS

Basically, Moses led the children of Israel all alone, without any real friends. Even his own family sometimes worked at odds with him. There was only God to stand with him. Single parents all too often feel like Moses, utterly alone, misunderstood, and blamed by others—even their own children—for the circumstances in which they find themselves.

There is hope for you as there was for Moses. The same Jesus who guided him will guide you, if you are willing. Perhaps no parent is more blessed in going up the mountain than the single parent who can there find empathy for their troubles, and equally importantly, a challenging, adult conversation and friendship with the King of kings. He doesn't hold the fact that you're a single parent against you. He's waiting, even now, for you to climb up the mountain to be with Him.

Chapter 6

PUTTING ON THE BRAKES

"In returning and rest shall ye be saved; in quietness and confidence shall be your strength: and ye would not" (Isaiah 30:15).

"*L*ord I'm—"

"Sally?" Jim's voice interrupts my thoughts. "Have you seen my dark gray suit?"

"Oh Jim, I'm sorry! We got home so late from town I must have accidentally left it in the car after picking it up at the cleaners. I'll go see if I can find it." Sure enough, the suit is hanging in the back of the car. As I carry it in, I feel bad for Jim having to put on this freezing cold suit. I place it near the stove and take a minute to kindle a fire to warm it up. But it's all for nothing because Jim doesn't have time to wait for it. I return to my thoughts and prayers, feeling bad about forgetting.

"Lord, I am so pressed. My life is so full. I feel that I just can't take it any longer. My thoughts are turning to mush from so many things pushing themselves into my mind—my jobs, my lists, and my family. It's enough to—"

"Mother?" It's Andrew this time. He has come downstairs and is starting breakfast. My head swirls to meet yet another distraction. I deal with Andrew's need.

Back to my prayer. "Lord, I'm honestly doing my best. I've increased my efficiency dramatically, as well as my speed, and still I can't get done with all the seemingly important things that funnel themselves into my day! I live in the wilderness, so how can my life be so busy? What am I to do? Oh, excuse me, Lord, I have to answer the telephone."

Returning from the phone call, quietness is slow to return to my mind, and I sit there without a notable word from God. No solution, no communication, nothing to resolve my troubles. So . . . more than a little put off, I get up to return to my never-ending duties. "Not enough time, never enough time," I mutter, feeling very sorry for myself.

My thoughts run on in the same vein as I work. "Why is God putting all this on my plate?" I ask myself. "Does He expect me to work this hard and long without a break, without even sufficient time to get an answer from Him? Must everything be done in a hurry?" I actually feel irritated with God for being so unreasonable. I am being logical and rational as I conclude that God must be unfair, yet that conclusion doesn't sit too well. Intuitively I feel God *isn't* unfair or unreasonable, and yet, my questions are reasonable and deserve an answer. I reconsider the things that occupy my time and conclude there is nothing that was bad or wrong with them; there are just too many! Surely God is as smart and reasonable as I am. If I can see that I have too much to do, then He knows it too—and He wouldn't ask me to do too much. I felt much better about this conclusion, but it led me to another question: If God isn't putting all this work and all these burdens on me, who is?

"Lord, somewhere I read that if I do only those things necessary for running my household and caring for my family that I should have sufficient time to read my Bible and perfect my character through You. Well, my experience doesn't bear this out. My character development is consistently at the bottom of my list of things to do—not for lack of desire, but for lack of enough time. It gets crowded out along with everything else. I'm trying to shape Matthew's and Andrew's characters, and that seems to take every minute I have. Then, in addition to that, I have to help all the ladies that call me for help with their children. After all it is the Christian thing to do. Then I help with the social activities at the church—because they ask me to. I plan the lessons for the children's division at church—because that is my job. Plus I make all my food from scratch and home school my boys besides. I don't want to complain, but I don't have enough time. I run all day long, every day! Superwoman would have trouble accomplishing these feats, and I'm not superwoman! I'm just Sally-woman, and I'm tired Lord!"

"Are you sure I want you to do all those things?" His still, small voice questioned.

"Well, what should I eliminate—the laundry, the ironing, the cooking, the cleaning, or maybe even stop doing the dishes?" I said defensively.

"If you do only those things that are necessary, Sally . . . is everything necessary? Is there anything you can change?"

I thought of some texts I had read, especially one that said, "In returning and rest shall ye be saved" (Isaiah 30:15). Rest jumped out at me; it was my need. My thoughts turned to Mary, Jesus' mother. She wasn't involved in excessive church work—or any other work—that kept her from her first work. Others didn't raise her Jesus. In fact, she and Joseph had been forced to spend some of the most formative years of Jesus' life in a foreign country, removed from associations, family influences, and distractions. Even after they returned to their homeland, Mary isn't portrayed as ministering to others until after Christ was a grown man. Her priorities matched her use of time. This gave me some things to contemplate.

We all have twenty-four hours, and that is all we have. It is up to me to make time for the things I see as important. God doesn't want circumstances to chase me wildly. We need to put on the brakes to determine where we are and where we want to go—rather than continuing to go in the direction and at the pace that we are!

"Lord, I've considered what You said. I'm sorry I got defensive with You. Now I see a few things I can change." I decided I could lessen my laundry time by having my family not just throw every item in the wash, but evaluate whether it is really dirty. Reusing an acceptably clean pair of pants or a shirt wouldn't sacrifice true cleanliness, and it would save me a lot of laundry time—almost half. The more I thought about it the more sense this made. I began to wonder what else I could do.

"I forgive you Sally. You are doing well to evaluate whether everything you're doing is necessary. Do only those necessary things."

"God, are You saying that I don't need to do everything I'm doing?" This thought floored me. "That must mean that not everything I'm asked to do is from You. Oh how I need divine wisdom from You to determine what things I should eliminate from my life! I need time with You to know the difference between what's needful and what isn't. You aren't asking me to be superwoman after all? Then it must be Satan keeping me from my work of character building."

"Sally, you need to learn to say 'No' gracefully at the right time. Every phone call is not from Me. Every need is not yours to supply. Every crying child is not yours to correct. Every church duty is not yours to fill. You need to find the balance in all these areas. Seek Me and filter the demands on your time through Me to find the balance you desire."

"Saying 'No' is so hard for me, Lord. Help me to learn!"

God did help me, although not quite in the way I expected. With great glee, Jim actually had me go out on the front porch and practice saying "No"! He had me begin by saying "No" softly. Then in a moderate tone. Then more firmly. Then very firmly. And finally by saying, "No, thank you. I'm not available this time." I practiced, feeling very silly. But Jim helped me see that I was to run school and the home as my business. During business hours I would not be distracted from my focus. If I succumb to distractions, my children's education gets crowded out or crippled. So from then on, when someone called and wanted to visit, I told them, "I can't talk with you right now, but if you call me later, we can talk then." It worked. Most people understood because they struggled with the same issues. God gave me discernment when to say Yes and No. If you have trouble saying "No," try practicing it out loud on your front porch. It's a little embarrassing, at first, but it helps when weak moments come—and they will come!

Is there so much in your life, as there was in mine, that God and your children's character development are crowded out? If so, it is not by accident. It is the plan of the enemy of our souls to keep us overly busy and distracted until it is forever too late. Development of a godly character doesn't just happen. If so, we all would be a lot more like

Him. Raising children to follow and serve Christ is almost extinct on our planet today because to do so involves heart work, not just an outward obedience or outward appearance of sweetness. To experience the personal indwelling of Christ changing the heart is a thing rarely sought even among those who claim to follow Him; even more rare is it to find one who has actually entered into this practically or consistently. The result is that we settle for outward forms of Christianity—ceremony, display, outward smiling, and outward obedience—that replace the true work of Christ in the heart.

Character is everything. Character is our inner thoughts, feelings, and motives. Our daily lives determine our destiny, as minute by minute, time slips through our fingers almost unnoticed. Are we addressing practical character development in our children, or is the opportunity slipping away from us? Time bears us along, and the moments become years, and then they, too, slip away, seeming to move faster with every passing day like a runaway train on a steep grade.

If you want something different for yourself and your children, you must begin, right now, to put on the brakes. It may seem impossible because of all your tasks and responsibilities and the momentum they create, but you can have a heaven-ordained balance in your life by seeking God and connecting with Him. How would God order your priorities? God wants to create you into His image. He wants you to have sufficient time with Him. All power to change your character and home is based upon this connection. Second after God, comes your spouse, and your family is third. Everything else comes after that, including your employment. A thousand things invite our attention and consume our time, ending in nothing of lasting importance. We have everything good to gain by taking our foot off the accelerator and putting on the brakes.

As God began making this clear to me, I said, "OK, Lord, but how can I know what to omit from my schedule and what to keep? Why, I have a hard time discarding excess clothing in my closet; how can I sort out these important things?"

"Sally, many activities can be judged by asking, 'Is this a call from man or a call from Me?'"

I understood this concept from the way we had to deal with calls for our speaking ministry. But it was a new thought to apply it to my work in the home and with my children.

We get far more requests for speaking engagements than we can possibly fill. When we started, Jim said, "Sally, if we take every call we get, we will lose our health in overwork. Even if we don't, running that much would surely crowd out our time with Jesus—and then who would be leading us? Whom would we be sharing from the pulpit—Christ or self?"

We decided God didn't want us to overwork and crowd Him out. Even when faced with good opportunities, we need to let God lead and maintain balance. Of course, Satan wants to coax us into overdoing, so he tries to make us feel guilty for not accepting every invitation. But God wants us to take personal responsibility for managing our lives logically and thoughtfully, consulting with Him at every step. It's our choice—either to do a few things well or many things poorly. This process of saying yes or no as God leads is putting on the brakes and slowing down our out-of-control lives.

And that is just what we did. God led us to find the right balance for who we were at that time in our lives. It's a balance that continues to change as we change. We can't look to other similar ministries for guidance in this. Another brother or sister may do more or less than I. So it is not good to compare ourselves amongst ourselves. We had to learn what God wanted for Jim and Sally, and you will have to learn what God wants for you. Human beings give input and options, but the final decision comes down to God and you. Is every call to ministry from Heaven? Don't make an immediate decision. Pray for guidance. Talk out your options with your spouse. Allow yourself time to look at the total picture so that you don't just continue to add good things to your load until you've reached the breaking point. You are not wrong to prevent a broken family through lack of balance.

When I considered "putting on the brakes," I knew I needed to gain time to invest in character development, both personally and in my children. I thought and thought and at last realized my largest time consumer is home schooling. That's where I feel pressure because even with all the time I spend in this area, there is never enough time to do it all. *"Sally, My dear child, you must first consider whether you have a bent to excess. Do you remember how many subjects you wanted your first-grader to do?"*

I couldn't help but laugh out loud. "Yes, Lord, I remember. I chose eleven subjects. But I did eventually give up three of them. And they were all good subjects—things I wanted to cover!

"Okay, Sally, let's reason this through. Are all these subjects feasible, practically speaking? How much time do you need for each subject?"

I thought it through. "Well, at one hour per subject . . . that would be eleven hours of our day." *Eleven hours!* I had never thought of it this way. If I'd had my way, there wouldn't have been time for anything else—like taking care of my house, cooking, play, in fact nothing! "It's no wonder I'm frustrated! I'm trying to get too much done. Even my present eight hours per day is too much—way too much—for a first-grader. I'm unbalanced. Lord, no wonder I get frustrated and never finish. I'm attempting to do the impossible."

God led me to a balance that was right for me. I decided to do a few subjects well. I settled on five basic subjects. Each subject was well mastered. Words cannot sufficiently express the joy that came into our school program when it was balanced in Jesus. The pressures I had artificially placed on all of us disappeared. We all had time for God and each other. Pruning is good when God has the pruning knife and balance is achieved.

You may not be involved in home schooling as I was, but all of us find ourselves in something. Evaluate your time and whether you are using it for character development. Do you have time to talk with God—and time to wait for His answer? Where is your excess? What consumes your last energies of the day and crowds out the more important things? Go to your Helper and find your balanced answer.

When I began to evaluate my time expenditures, it didn't take long to remove the bad things and the excesses out of my life. However, I found God's pruning knife challenging me in things that were not necessarily bad, but which were crowding out the best. It's like caring for a garden. Weeding is not enough. I must thin the good, healthy plants, sacrificing some to allow others to mature and bear fruit. In the same way, don't be afraid to evaluate all your activities—even good ones. Let God apply His pruning knife, and you will find an even greater peace.

Once I started making these changes, Jesus taught me another precious truth about time management. *"Sally, you need to learn the art of subtraction. You already have a full plate, right? So you can't add to your life, unless you also subtract from it. When someone comes to add anything to your day, you must consider what you will subtract in order to do it."*

Not long afterward, I got a request to help prepare a community meal. I thought about it before saying "yes" or "no." I realized it would require two nights of preparation plus helping in the kitchen the night of the dinner. Using my new method of addition and subtraction, I considered what I'd have to subtract to accommodate this new request. I'd have to subtract our evening family fun time and family worship for three nights. The choice was clear—I must say "No," and so I did.

Don't think that this program means always saying "No." One day I got a request from a camping group, wondering if I could supervise the children for two hours while the parents had a meeting. This request was scheduled during our free time and family fun time. We decided to turn this event into a family hike and entertain the children at the same time. It would be a nice social event for the boys and a fun outing for all of us. We decided that we could be home for family worship just a little later than usual, so nothing would be eliminated or crowded. We talked about it as a family, prayed about it, and responded positively that we *could* help.

God showed me that the art of subtraction went even further. He wanted to use it to develop skills and attitudes in my children that they would need for productive, happy lives. He prompted me like this.

"Sally, subtraction can also lessen your work load in the home by calling upon your children to carry more responsibility according to their age and ability. You need to teach your children how to bear their share of life's burdens in the practical duties of life in order to subtract from the responsibilities you carry."

"Getting my children to do household chores isn't easy. They will fuss and grumble. It's easier and faster to do it myself, Lord."

"You have too much on your plate. You're frustrated and tired from too much work. Isn't that what you've been asking Me to help you with? This is your solution. Try it."

I had been considering hiring a maid to help me, but I needed to try God's solution first. I soon found the opportunity to call my children in from play to help me fold clothes. I had to face their unwilling dispositions, but God led me through this scenario, and they helped fold the clothes with happy hearts. It was the beginning of an ever-increasing freedom for me. And what better way can we prepare our children for taking responsibility as adults? As they mastered individual tasks, I put them in charge of all the laundry or all the meals for the day or all the daily housekeeping. They found that joy comes from doing a good job; they gained confidence that they could carry even heavier responsibilities. The art of subtraction is for our children's good and for their pleasure.

Putting on your brakes will require you to alter your life in such a way that many people will think you are out of touch with the mainstream. They may misunderstand your motives and try to convince you of your errors. In fact, few who have not traveled this road can appreciate, or even comprehend, the rewards and lasting joys that await those who accept the apparent self-denial involved in letting go even of good things so that they may have the best. As one who has traveled this road for some time, I assure you that under God's direction, it is the best and only route to lasting happiness and peace.

THE LONE EMBRACE
A SPECIAL WORD OF ENCOURAGEMENT FOR SINGLE PARENTS

I know that throughout this book I have been telling you hard things—and you have borne up admirably. Now, at last, you get the chance to discard a few items on your "to do" list. Of all people, you deserve the opportunity to find a little extra time. Don't be afraid to think "outside the box" of other's expectations. You're not depriving your children when you preserve the time needed for a happy and peaceful home. Work with your children to redeem time for things they really want to do.

Be sure your children see a return on their investment. If they must help, be sure that at least a portion of that time is returned in extra attention and fun with mother. I have been astonished at the inventiveness of some single parents who manage to find all sorts of ways to redeem time for their children. Remember that God understands your circumstances; when you are doing what you can, He will supply the lack.

Chapter 7

MY WILL—HOW TO EXERCISE IT

"Submit yourselves therefore to God. Resist the devil, and he will flee from you"
(James 4:7).

"Sally, I'm supposed to do special music for church on the eighteenth. Would you be willing to sing a duet with me?" Sherry asked hopefully.

"Oh Sherry, the last time we did that I went flat."

"You were just nervous. You'll do fine this time," she said reassuringly.

"I don't know, Sherry. I, I—I'll have to get back to you." I quickly hung up the phone, my thoughts racing. "I just can't do it, Lord! Just the memory of it makes me blush. I got up there, and the fear just overwhelmed me. I couldn't remember my part properly, could hardly croak out a sound; it was terrible. I was so humiliated. Lord, You don't want me to sing with her, do you?"

"Yes, I would like you to. What hinders you, Sally?"

"What hinders me! Well, I—I'm just not able to sing.

"Sally, I know you can sing."

I knew my statement wasn't entirely true, so I tried again. "Lord, you know I love to sing—to You—privately. I just can't sing in front of people. I fall apart. I'm afraid I'll go flat, and then I do! My knees knock together. I'm afraid I'll forget the words, even though I practice excessively, and sure enough I forget them!"

"So, you are afraid then?"

"Hmm—I've never labeled it that way before, but yes."

"What are you afraid of?"

"Well, I'm afraid of people. When I look at their faces, I just come unglued."

"What is in their faces that makes you afraid?"

I wasn't sure where the Lord was going with all these thoughts, but I finally responded, "They might reject me. I'm afraid they will think I'm stupid or unworthy of being up front. What if they tell me to sit down? I would just die of embarrassment."

"What happens when you get so nervous before you sing?"

"Lord, You know I get terrible butterflies in my stomach. My throat gets so tight, I'm afraid I won't be able to sing a note. I get so nervous looking at the people. Jim tells me to sing to You and to look at the ceiling instead of the audience. It helps a little, but I still *know* they are there!"

"The next time you sing, give Me those butterflies. I can take them away, and then you can sing well. Your butterflies simply represent your fears. 'Be not afraid of their faces: for I am with thee to deliver thee' (Jeremiah 1:8). 'There is no fear in love; but perfect love casteth out fear; because fear hath torment' " (1 John 4:18).

"I know by experience that fear is a torment, but do You mean I can get rid of my fears? That sounds wonderful, but how?"

No answer followed this time.

I finally realized that He had *already* told me what to do. The key was in that little word *give*. I made up my mind to try it.

With much trepidation, I called Sherry and told her I'd sing with her. But when the time actually came, I wondered if I had lost my senses. "Why am I here?" I wondered. My knees were weak and shaky. I just knew I would go flat or forget the words. All my instincts screamed for me to flee! As if on cue, the butterflies added to my dilemma.

In the midst of this internal storm, God tapped me on the shoulder, so to speak, with the thought: *"Sally, do you want to give those butterflies to Me?"*

"Oh that would be wonderful! Yes, yes, yes! You may have them; here they all are." Yet I still felt them. They were still there! "Excuse me, Lord, but I think You forgot to take them?"

"I'll take them; trust Me. You need to relax like a mother in childbirth."

"Relax, relax . . . OK, relax. I'll relax my shoulders because they feel really tight." Within a few minutes my butterflies were gone, my throat was free, and my hopes began to grow. "This is great, Lord. Thanks."

Sherry and I threaded our way up the aisle to sing, and the butterflies immediately returned! "This isn't supposed to happen, Lord," I cried inwardly as I struggled to sing. I went flat a little, but not as bad as many times before.

As I paused for breath, I heard that still small voice say, *"Sally, give Me those butterflies. I'll take them again. Trust Me."*

"You can have them, Lord. Please take them from me. They are Yours." Again, the butterflies subsided enough for me to continue. I looked at the ceiling and sang to Jesus, trying with all my might to erase the faces from my mind and to see only Jesus. This was the best I'd ever done in public! God was indeed my Helper in time of need.

Later as I reflected on this experience, I began to reason, "My will is simply my choice. I can choose what I am going to think, say, do, or even feel. My feelings are not my will. Every moment, the choice is mine." Reading my Bible, I came to James 4:7—"Submit yourselves therefore to God. Resist the devil, and he will flee from you."

That's it! That's what I have been doing wrong! I've been resisting the devil *alone,* and he hasn't been fleeing from me because I'm not connected to Jesus who has the authority. The devil won't flee from *me.* I need to follow the order of this text—first submit myself to God and be willing to trust what He says. When I choose to follow Jesus, I have His power. The devil will flee from me because Jesus tells him he must leave. That's it! When I try to fight these fears by myself, I fail because I'm doing it out of order, without Christ. If I choose *with my will* to submit to Jesus and give Him the butterflies and fears, I have victory because Jesus tells the devil he must leave. And when I forget to trust, or choose not to, the butterflies come right back because Satan doesn't obey Sally without Jesus. That must be why I have this on-and-off experience. I want to learn to be continually connected to Jesus.

When I choose to cooperate and think right thoughts, Jesus creates right feelings in me, too, and these new thoughts and feelings work together to form a new character in the image of God. Then I can respond rightly, not because of any good in me, but because God is transforming my thoughts and feelings, planting trust in place of fear.

No matter who you are, what your baggage is, what wrong habits you carry, or what poor problem-solving skills you possess, this simple exercise of the human will, cooperating with divine wisdom and direction, will work for you. You *can* change. Once you understand the power of the will from a practical point of view, you can teach it to your children. The ability to properly exercise the will is perhaps the most important legacy we can give our children!

For years, I thought the exercise of my will was me trying to stuff down wrong thoughts, words, and deeds, but let me assure you, it doesn't work any better than trying to sing in church with butterflies in your stomach. It's like trying to seal off a boiling pot of water. It never works, and the wrong spirit, like the boiling water, somehow finds a way to spurt out—usually at the worst possible moment.

"Apart from Me," the Lord said, *"you are in the flesh, and every such effort must fail! Trying to give the right appearance outwardly without dealing with the inward heart may appear proper, but it's impure on the inside—the heart. I look on the heart. If you let Me cleanse your heart—your wrong thoughts and feelings—then your frustration will be gone, not merely hidden. Then you are clean within and without. You need to understand more than you do how to surrender your will to Me."*

"I think I see. So stuffing down my frustration in self is *I* fighting the sin, and every such effort must fail. My will is not to fight the sin, but rather it's to be exercised to surrender the wrong, the sin, to You to slay, evict, or subdue. With my cooperation, You subdue and replace frustrations with care and sympathy while I'm trusting. When my heart is cleansed of frustrations by You, the attitude and behavior of frustration no longer exists because care and sympathy exist in their place, influencing these different feelings and responses. You want me clean within, so that I'm truly clean outwardly. My example now becomes worthy of imitation. You don't want pretentious, outward behavior, but the real thing that You work from the inside out. I like that!"

Soon I had the opportunity to exercise my will in a very tangible way.

Have you ever had one of those mornings where everything seems gloomy and almost any comment can really rub you the wrong way? Well, I was having one of those mornings, and my husband had supplied the wrong comment that morning before breakfast. Now I was ironing, and if you could have seen the expression on my face, you could easily have read my thoughts. I was busily rehashing those hurtful words Jim had spoken. He had offended me, and I was busy having my own little pity party—and getting sadder by the moment.

"Sally, you can choose to be happy," the Lord whispered.

"What do You mean, Lord? Be happy with such an insensitive man for a husband? You've got to be kidding me!"

"The choice to be happy or sad is yours. You can choose to be happy, if you will. I'm here to help you."

"I don't feel happy, Lord. You know what Jim said to me. You probably want me to be happy and smile, and then You'll change me inside and make it real, right? Well, I don't know if I even want to."

"Sally, the only person you're hurting is you. Let Me have the sadness, and I'll give you My happiness."

"So I can put on a plastic smile and be Sally Christian?" I fussed. So I pasted on a smile by sheer human muscle power. It lasted about five seconds. "I'm just a phony. It isn't real. I feel sad. Besides, I want Jim to see what he has done! Pretending to be happy makes me feel like a hypocrite, and I won't be a hypocrite. I am what I am."

"Why don't you sing the happy song and let Me have those ill feelings?"

"But I'm comfortable being sad. I'm used to it. Besides it makes me feel better to rehearse Jim's faults. Then I'm justified feeling the way I do."

Of course, I knew I shouldn't be thinking and acting this way, but it was how I felt. The Lord didn't argue with me; He just waited until the angry emotions started to die down, which they did a few moments later. I started to think that I *did* want to obey God and that I *had* asked

Him this morning to keep me in His path. "OK, Lord—all my sadness is Yours to subdue. But the song? The happy song? What happy song? Oh, I remember." It was a short little chorus I had learned not that long ago. So I sang, "I'm very happy, I'm very happy. I'm very happy, happy, happy, happy . . ." As I sang, I felt like the biggest fake there ever was because I didn't feel happy. But I continued, "I'm very happy, I'm very happy. Jesus saved me from . . . my . . . sins!"

"Oh, this is sin, Lord!"

Yes, but in Me, I'll subdue it. (See Hebrews 2:8.)

I sang the song a second time. A third time. And by the fourth time I was truly, whole-heartedly happy from the inside out! Jesus performed this miracle in me because I gave the wrong to Him to subdue and co-operated with His power. "Thank you, Lord! I love my Jim; he is such a good husband!"

The exercise of my will consisted first in *choosing* to let God subdue the sadness in me and second in *cooperating* with Him by singing the happy song as He asked me to do. Scripture says, "Behold, I am the Lord, the God of all flesh: is there anything too hard for me?" (Jeremiah 32:27). "Only that which I do not give You!" I responded.

We want our children to choose to obey us. But to train our children how to surrender their wills to us, to God, and to do right, we parents ourselves need to know by practical experience how to surrender our wills to God.

"Lord, help me rightly understand Joshua 24:15," I prayed. "It says, 'Choose you this day whom ye will serve; whether the gods which your fathers served that were on the other side of the flood—' " I stopped there. "What 'gods' is this talking about?" I asked. "Adam and Eve were on the other side of the flood, and Eve served her feelings and appetites. Then these other gods must include appetite and feeling," I reasoned.

I continued reading the verse. " 'Or the gods of the Amorites, in whose land ye dwell.' Who are the gods of the Amorites? Well, the Amorites served worldliness, fleshly emotions, perverted inclinations, desires, and wants. Then these, too, were other 'gods.' "

I completed the text, " 'but as for me and my house, we will serve the Lord.' The 'Lord' is the God of heaven. Like the Israelites at Jordan, we have important choices to make. I want the *real* God, not a false god."

Looking at the chart that follows will help us see what Joshua labeled as other gods. It will help us distinguish between the false and the true and the voice of God from the voice of the flesh. This chart will help us understand what choices we need to make—for and against.

MAN
Higher Powers—Based on the Word of God

the Spirit communicated
Through the . . .

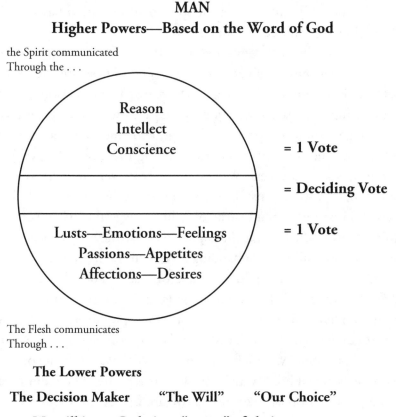

Reason
Intellect
Conscience

= 1 Vote

= Deciding Vote

Lusts—Emotions—Feelings
Passions—Appetites
Affections—Desires

= 1 Vote

The Flesh communicates
Through . . .

The Lower Powers

The Decision Maker   **"The Will"**   **"Our Choice"**

My will is my God-given "power" of choice
My will is the governing power in the nature of man
The will casts the deciding vote!

Adapted illustration courtesy of Ty Gibson copyright 1986 Light Bearers. Used with permission.

Two forces influence us greatly: the higher powers and the lower powers. The higher powers are that part of us through which God's Holy Spirit communicates—our reason, intellect, and conscience. This is where Christ needs to reign. Everything starts in the mind! When a decision needs to be made, God works through these avenues to suggest a better, higher way than our present course, and thus the higher powers cast one vote. Not every thought is of divine origin, of course, but if we are willing to listen, God does speak though these avenues, offering us ideas about what we should do. God is never demanding, but He offers His guidance in the spirit of a suggestion based on His Word, leaving you free to choose.

The lower powers communicate through our feelings, emotions, appetites, passions, inclinations, and desires. These are the avenues Satan seeks to use to influence our decisions. There is nothing wrong with having feelings and emotions; God gave them to us. He wants us to have good healthy appetites, feelings, and emotions. Satan, on the other hand, perverts our appetites, pushing them outside God-given boundaries and to excess. When our lower powers are perverted and indulged, they war against the higher powers. When we face a decision, they also cast a vote, but instead of politely suggesting what we should do, as God does through the higher powers, they often behave like undisciplined children, demanding their own way.

Our will is in the middle of these two centers of influence, as the chart illustrates. It is like a judge—judging between good and evil. It hears both sides, and it consults with the Holy Spirit to decide which way we are going to go. The will casts the *deciding vote,* and that is why it is so very important. We are free to choose which way we will go, which set of powers will hold sway in our lives irrespective of circumstances, feelings, or emotions. Like Joshua, we are free before God to choose whom we will serve.

I think that's wonderful! It means I don't have to obey Satan, no matter how much he tempts or pushes me. It means I don't have to obey my feelings of fear that make me get the butterflies when I want to sing or the thoughts that tell me I'm stupid and unworthy. Putting my will on God's side gives power to my choices—all the power of heaven.

The war to choose commences the moment we rise each day. I can choose whether to trust God to subdue the lower powers or whether to allow them to control me. It's my choice, but the power to carry out such a choice comes from God alone. It explains the miracle of having the butterflies subdued so that I can sing; it explains my ability to be happy when I'm inclined to be sad. Both victories occurred by choosing Christ's side and receiving His power. God can transform any wrong I give to Him. This is how God re-creates us into His image.

As a teenager, I drove some big trucks. Steering them takes the strength of a sumo wrestler. No way could I, of myself, steer those trucks for very long; my strength was insufficient. That's just how it felt sometimes trying to steer my flesh, my lower powers. I'm not capable of steering around tight corners for very long before it gets out of control. Connecting with God is like adding hydraulic power steering to those big, old trucks. Even little Sally, weak as I am, can drive one of those semi-trucks with hydraulic power steering. It isn't any trouble to keep it under control around the tightest corner. We need God's "hydraulics" to steer our fleshly nature, too!

When Adam and Eve fell into sin and chose their own will over God's, the seeds for disobedience were sown. This is our heritage, passed down generation after generation and deteriorating steadily. After sin entered the human family, our natural inclination—our human will—brings us automatically under the control of Satan—as long as we are unaided by divine power. Our will is in Satan's hands, and we obey him by thinking his thoughts and feeling his feelings. As a result, we demonstrate his character. This is why we so naturally serve selfishness today and why we are so weak when it comes to trying to do right.

Even our free will, that great divine blessing of free choice, has been so damaged by exposure to sin that unless it is enlightened by God's

Spirit, we tend to choose wrongly. Our inclination to evil is both our heritage and a cultivated habit. We must put our will into Jesus' hands in order to choose against Satan, the prince of this world. Jesus will cleanse our will and return it to us purified. Unless I learn to put myself under Christ's control today, moment by moment, I'm automatically under Satan's control. There truly is no middle ground.

When we moved to Montana, we were living very frugally on meager finances. We went to town only once a month. Now when you go that rarely, your list of places to go and things to do is very long. Jim and I learned to be efficient with our errands by covering one section of the town at a time and splitting up our tasks. Working together, we had a lovely spirit. When we weren't working together—well, see how the story unfolds.

"Jim, I need to go to three places in this area. If you drop me off here, you can pick me up over there. How long will you be?"

"Well Sally, I need to go to the license bureau; that will take forty-five minutes. Oh, and I need you to drop off this book at the library and pick up the book I have on hold there before you go to your other stops. You'll still have plenty of time."

That is when it happened! Self did not want to surrender this time!

"But Jim, I don't want to go to the library! You'll just have to go when I'm somewhere else. I don't like going to the library; you know that!"

Jim, the rascal, just pulled up to the curb by the library, handed me the book, and smiled. "Of all the nerve," I thought, "expecting me to do his errand." I refused even to look at him. I opened the car door, got out, and closed the door nicely. I didn't slam it! I didn't vent angry words. But I was irritated. I looked okay on the outside, but was I surrendered to God's will? Not at all! Not to decide is to decide. I was automatically exercising my will to do wrong, just by following my inclination to resent him.

"That Jim, he always gets his way!" I fumed to myself as I crossed the road to the library. "I don't like going to the library, and he knows it! I don't know why I don't like going there, but I just don't! Jim is the problem, not my peculiarities, even if they don't have a valid reason."

"Sally, it's a little thing." God spoke gently to my conscience.

"Little thing? Little thing? No, it's *not* a little thing! This is a big thing."

As I walked up the steps to the library, God whispered, *"Sally, this isn't a good way to go. You know where this kind of thinking leads. You can choose for it to be a little thing. I'm here to make it so."*

The lower powers quickly cast their vote by compelling my thoughts and feelings. "I don't want to!" "Jim's always in charge!" "This isn't fair! He's going to one place while I'm going to four places!" All these were excuses, trying to justify my ill feelings.

The higher powers also cast their vote by suggesting to my reason, intellect, and conscience, "It's a little thing." "This is something nice you can do for Jim." "He's not *that* bad!" I exercised my will in each case by not actively choosing Christ's way. In that way, I chose to go along with the current of thoughts from the lower powers. Every time we choose not to decide for Christ and right, we have decided.

I returned the book and waited in line to get the book on hold. I continued in the same vein, thinking about every negative thing Jim had ever done—real or supposed—and I felt quite justified in my course.

"Sally, you're not even happy. You know the longer you persist in this thinking, the harder it is to turn away from it. Do you really want to continue? I can help you."

The Lord finally got through my passions, and I realized that much of what I had been thinking about Jim was stretching the truth pretty far just to make me feel justified for being mad at him. Jim is a good man, and I knew it. "No, Lord, I don't want to continue in this way. Jesus, I need You to steer me out of this state of mind. I give You my will to change it. I don't want Satan's rule. I want You to make me Your child again." When I exercised my will and chose rightly, peace flowed back into my heart. But I still had a lot of negative feelings floating around.

4—P.B.T.S.

The Lord knew this and prompted me. *"You need to stop thinking negatively about Jim, and think positively."*

"Okay, Lord, let's think positively. Let me think of something good about Jim. Something good about Jim? Hmm, surely there is something good about Jim. I know there is something good about Jim, but I can't think of anything! Oh Lord, can You help me? Thinking all those negative thoughts has just crowded out all the good from my mind."

"Remember how Jim gives you all those hugs and kisses at the computer, the kitchen sink, or anywhere—for no reason other than to make you feel loved?"

"Oh yes, how could I ever forget? He is so much fun at work or play. Life is boring without Jim. He even picked me a bouquet of wild flowers recently." It was difficult for me to change the direction of my thoughts, but God cleansed them of all the negativity and returned them to me purified. I was much happier for this choice. I really had been miserable serving self.

What do you suppose my response to Jim would have been if he had picked me up while I was still thinking all this negative stuff about him? No matter what he would have said, I would have been offended, on the defensive, silent, or critical—right? As Satan's subject, I could demonstrate only his character traits. We respond the way we do because of who we are following and what we are thinking.

What do you think happened when Jim picked me up after his trip to the license bureau? Well, by that time, I had only love in my thoughts and feelings. I greeted him cheerily with a kiss and a hug. I told him of my struggles in the library and of my final triumph when I exercised my will and chose God's side. There was no distance between us, no quiet reserve on my part, no resentment or animosity against him for sending me to the library. In Jesus, it had indeed become a "little thing" because I chose to let it be one and followed God's leading out of negative thinking.

When I gave God permission to re-create my will, He did a mighty work in me. Paul in 2 Corinthians 10:4, 5 says, "(For the weapons of our warfare are not carnal, but mighty through God) . . . Casting down imaginations, and every high thing . . . and bringing into captivity every thought to the obedience of Christ." "Be strengthened with might by his Spirit in the inner man" (Ephesians 3:16). This is what God wants for you and me.

But we must daily continue to turn our thoughts over to God's control. One day I took my boys for a walk in the mountains. Jim couldn't go with us. We had walked only about two minutes when I was struck with fear. "What might happen if a bear came out of the woods right over there?" I thought to myself. Suddenly fear swelled up in my emotions like a terrible storm. I hadn't asked for it. I hadn't been thinking fearful thoughts or having gloomy forebodings—and yet, here they were! I had to deal with them somehow, but my mind flooded with negative facts. A bear can run forty miles an hour and goes from zero to full speed in moments. That wasn't exactly the comforting thought I needed right then!

I looked toward the cabin and thought, "I couldn't even run home before the bear would overtake me—especially with two little ones in hand." People say you should climb a tree to get away from a bear, but our trees here in Montana, at least the ones that were big enough to get away from a bear, were huge and limbless for at least the first ten feet. If I depended on getting up one of them to escape a bear, the tree wouldn't be the only thing limbless before long! It seemed that every tree hid a bear that would jump out and eat me. Jim had repeatedly told me, "God didn't bring us up here for a bear to eat you." But I wasn't so sure. Making it worse, I seldom see any kind of wild animal—bears, mountain lions, or deer—until Jim or the boys point them out to me. I imagined the bears taking great delight in leaping out to frighten me and then finishing off my trembling body at their leisure. I just knew they looked at my pink, city-softened flesh and saw a McSally happy meal, unhindered by horns, hoofs, or even fur. I wanted to run home and hide!

"Do you remember the text I gave you recently on the evil beasts in the woods?" God asked.

"Yes, I remember it. Ezekiel 34:24, 25. 'I the Lord will be their God, . . . I will make with them a covenant of peace, and will cause the evil beasts to cease out of the land: and they shall dwell safely in the wilderness, and sleep in the woods.' But, Lord, I find this text very hard to believe. You're saying that I should be able to lie down and go to sleep right here. That You would keep me safe from all the wild beasts. I hope you don't ask me to do *that*! I need to know what to do with my fears that are pushing me to run for home."

"Can you trust Me, Sally?" the Lord asked tenderly.

I struggled to answer this question. In church it's so easy to say we trust God, but out in the woods—that's another story. "Lord, what would You ask me to do if a bear came out of the woods right over there?" I asked, pointing to a place between myself and the house.

"If I asked you to go behind that tree over there, would you go?"

"What tree?" As I turned to look for the tree, I sensed clearly which tree God wanted me to see. I evaluated the size of that tree. It was wider than my hips, and I reasoned, "A bear's eyesight is poor, and God can make the wind blow in the opposite direction so he won't be able to smell us. I can stand behind that tree and put Matthew and Andrew behind me. Yes, I can trust You, Lord." Relief swept over me, and I asked, "I passed my test, didn't I, Lord? Can I go home now?"

"No Sally, I want you to go for that walk you planned. I will be with you. I want to teach you some more things."

"Oh no—this is such a hard thing! I don't know anyone who has been delivered from the kind of fear that I have. What can I do with all this fear?"

"Take My hand, and we will walk this walk together."

Full of fear, I made the choice against the pull of my flesh and walked in the opposite direction of my home, trusting Jesus could do something with my fears—although I didn't know what. I was scared to death that I would have to come face to face with a bear for this lesson. "Lord, my feet are obeying, but my thoughts are on my fears. What do I do with them?"

"Dwell on trusting and believing Me."

I began to sing and encouraged my boys to join me. I sang Scripture songs, hymns—anything that brought comfort or spoke of overcoming. I recited Bible texts: "Call upon me in the day of trouble: I will deliver thee, and thou shalt glorify me" (Psalm 50:15). "Perfect love casteth out fear" (1 John 4:18). "Fear thou not; for I am with thee: be not dismayed; for I am thy God: I will strengthen thee" (Isaiah 41:10). After five minutes, my fears were notably less, so we kept going. In another ten minutes, peace and trust presided where fear had once reigned. I returned home a victor, but it was not a one-time battle. As my fears returned, God used those opportunities to help me face my fear by choosing to place my will on His side, trusting Him, and seeing His salvation over and over. Overcoming my fears grew easier each time. Learning and training are important, yet the time comes to advance to the next level of growth with God. My graduation exercises came in a most interesting way.

We had heard of a mother bear with three cubs in our area, and in family worship the boys prayed we'd get a chance to see them. I added, "Let us see them safely, Lord." Sometimes our prayers are answered quickly. That very morning, as I was putting breakfast on the table, I saw a little, black bear cub outside our window! Then I saw the others—a mother and two more cubs. They were obviously black bears, easily differentiated from grizzly bears by their lack of a shoulder hump, the overall head shape, and by their smaller size—although smaller is a decidedly relative term! "Oh aren't they cute!" I exclaimed. We all watched them climb up and down a tree. Their performance convinced me of the futility of climbing a tree to escape a black bear! Then the mother put her nose in the air and began walking toward the back of our house. I knew what she wanted because I was making waffles with a double portion of vanilla. "I'll go close the back door," I thought to myself. The screen door had no latch, and even if it had one, it would never have slowed her down if she had wanted in.

When I got to the door, I just had to see what this bear was doing. I felt safe—after all, God had brought her. I opened the screen door and peeked out to see one, and then another, paw grasp the railing. Then with surprising grace for such a large creature, she seemed to just flow over the rail and onto the deck as though she visited houses every day! I let go of the screen, and it shut. But the inner door remained open; I stood transfixed in the doorway! She stood up on the other side of the screen, two feet taller than I was and only an arm's length away! "Oh, aren't you beautiful!" I breathed. I looked at her closely and motioned to the boys to come see her. They didn't, but I was too fascinated to pay much attention.

"You're drooling!" I exclaimed. "You want my waffles! You can't have them! You have such huge shoulders! I can see how you easily climb those tall mountains. Oh, look at those claws; they must be three inches long!" Her paws hung down in such a dainty, polite manner that she reminded me of a house pet.

It was with sadness that I watched her leave. Only then did I turn to my family and ask, "Why didn't you come and see her?"

The boys just looked at me in awe, and at last Jim said, "Sally, are you all right?"

I hadn't thought of it until then, but I'd had no fear of that bear! What was I doing? There had been only a screen door between us! I had acted as though Jesus had full charge of my life—and He did! I had nothing to fear from this great beast. Satan found no fear left in me to stir up. God had removed every bit of it. "Miracle of miracles, I'm free!" I exclaimed. "I'm free!" And while I can't prove it, I know my Jesus smiled at that moment.

Your task is to yield your will to the will of Jesus, and as you do this, God will immediately take possession and work in you to will and to do of His good pleasure. Your whole nature will then be brought under the control of the Spirit of Christ; even your thoughts will be subject to Him. You can't control your impulses or emotions as you may desire, but you can control your will, and this will make an entire change in your life. But our will must cooperate with God's will for this miracle to be ours.

Some sincere Christians have told me that a supernatural element will be brought into our lives in the future to lift us out of self into a higher sphere. They have said that overcoming sin will then be comparatively easy—no crucifixion of self. In fact they claim that struggling against self and the lower powers is legalism.

This is not reality. Of course, if we fought against sin in our own strength, they would be right. Our struggle would be a useless and losing battle from the start. But we have a God who offers us His power and salvation, not just in some future heavenly sphere, but right now. If we linger on Satan's ground, waiting for an easy victory at some future date, we will perish along with all evildoers. Sin retains its hold on us through our will. Without surrendering our will to Christ, we will not be delivered now or at some future time.

The true exercise of our will requires us to face our fears and weaknesses, letting Christ personally show us a way of escape. Trusting Jesus is a fearful thing in the beginning, but becomes an ever-sweeter experience as He severs the cords of sin and all the weaknesses that have held us in bondage for so long.

I opened this chapter telling about my fear when I would sing special music at church. God gave me many opportunities to face this fear. In the beginning, I just endured the butterflies because I was relying on self. But as I began to cooperate with God, I became much quicker to let Him have those butterflies. And the sooner I gave them to Him, the sooner I would have freedom from them. I began to wonder how often I would need to repeat this process. Why didn't they stay away for good? "Lord," I asked, "How many times do I have to give my butterflies to You before they are changed completely?"

"Until they are gone. Sooner or later—it varies."

A dear friend decided to get married and wanted me to sing at her wedding! She had no idea how I struggled with singing in public. I longed to do this for her as a special gift, but I just didn't know if I could. I didn't dare mess up her wedding! I told her I would pray about it and let her know.

I sought the Lord earnestly on my knees. "Lord, what should I do?" I cried in anguish. The answer was short and sweet.

"I think it would be lovely. I'll be with you."

"No, Lord, you don't know what You are asking!" After worrying about it a while, I consented, trusting God knew best. I picked out the most lovely, meaningful song I could find and practiced long, hard, and prayerfully. The day came, and I committed myself to God the best I knew how. I felt good, but a bit nervous. I was in the back pew when it happened. The butterflies swarmed into my stomach, worse than I had ever had them before. Doubts rushed in. "God isn't with you in this," I told myself, "you misread Him. He never gave you permission to do this, and Satan is going to get you real good now. You won't be able to sing, and you're going to ruin your friend's wedding!" The butterflies were so bad I doubled over, thinking maybe I was becoming severely ill. "Lord, what is happening? If You're not with me, I'm lost!" I cried out silently.

"I'm with you," the Lord lovingly reassured me. *"This is just those butterflies again—give them to Me."*

"This doesn't feel like any butterflies I remember! Are you sure?"

"Sally, trust me. Relax your muscles."

"Okay, Lord. I'm relaxing." And relax I did with all my will and might, trusting in Jesus to perform the real inner work. And sure enough the nervousness did lessen. However, the lower powers clamored to cast their vote—mocking me, telling me that God wasn't with me, that I was afraid and doomed to fail. My feelings confirmed these thoughts. Satan is the instigator of doubt; he loves to intimidate and discourage us. Seven times in the next fifteen minutes I gave those doubts and butterflies to God. Each time the butterflies got less and went away faster. The higher powers quietly encouraged me through my reason that God was indeed with me! I kept repeating Bible verses in my mind, but it wasn't an easy battle.

Soon it was my time to sing. Once more Satan stirred up feelings and emotions to make me doubt and lose confidence. God impressed me to hold on and endure once more.

I entered the battle doing all I knew and trustingly put myself in His hands. My throat was so tight I didn't think it could croak out a sound. My stomach cramped again as nervousness pressed me on all sides. "Lord I'm going up because You asked me to sing here. These fears are Yours to subdue, as only You can. I cast my helpless self upon You," I whispered and headed up the aisle to sing.

As I opened my mouth and sang, beautiful, harmonious music floated through the church. "Is this me?" I thought. I had perfect freedom in that song. My pitch, my breath control, my heart all came together as never before. It was wonderful. I was free! And their faces—I could look into each face without fear! "Praise God! Praise God!" I sang from my heart with perfect peace!

As I sang this marriage song to the couple for their wedding, I felt I was marrying Christ in a very tangible way and that He was freeing me from the last of these fears that held me hostage. I had thought to give my friend the gift of a beautiful song, and instead, God used her request to give me freedom to sing without fear. Never again have the butterflies attacked me that way! Never again was I afraid to look at their faces! Never again did I believe that I was incapable to sing up front! To God be the glory!

How often do we give our fears to Jesus? Until they are gone! So it may be with you!

THE LONE EMBRACE
A SPECIAL WORD OF ENCOURAGEMENT FOR SINGLE PARENTS

There is nothing in this chapter that a single parent cannot do. Many parents find themselves raising children alone—even when they have a spouse. The thing most likely to give you problems as you begin to change is the same thing I struggled with. No one wants to be viewed as the "mean" parent, especially when he or she feels badly about having to be away from the children all day at work. Parenting requires the objectivity to make hard choices, to deny what we would like for the greater good of our children, and to decide what is best for the long term rather than satisfying our desire for their immediate love and acceptance. Strive for balance in Jesus. The lack of a partner makes it much harder to face and refuse the selfish demands of your children who are often the only special people left in your life. That's why it is so important that Jesus become a very real and active part of your life. Time spent communing with God is not just a gift to yourself, but also to your child, who gains a parent better equipped to make the right choices—not simply give in because he or she is tired. Focus upon your relationship with Jesus, and He will lead you to make those changes you need in your specific circumstances.

Chapter 8

THE THOUGHT PUMP

"As [a man] thinketh in his heart, so is he" (Proverbs 23:7).

"Matthew, get back to bed right now!"

He stood there defiantly in the bedroom doorway. I had reasoned with him and read him the usual story. We'd been through drinks of water, lullabies, everything parents use to try to get their children settled into bed, and nothing was working! I tried discipline, and the more I did so, the more determined he became not to take his nap, and the angrier I became. In desperation, I finally plunked him into his bed and gave him a good scolding, shaking my finger all the while. "You're such a naughty boy! Now you lie down and sleep or else!" I had no idea what the "or else" would be, but I was at my wit's end and hoped the threat of some unknown punishment would scare him into obedience.

Silence reigned as I left the room and headed down the stairs. Ah, victory at last! I glanced back to savor my triumph—and there he was, peeking out the bedroom door at me!

I stomped back upstairs, "Matthew, you are not the one in charge; I am! I am the mother, and you are the child, and you are supposed to obey me—get it?" My two-year-old son didn't get it, and truthfully, neither did I. Why wouldn't my two-year-old obey me? Hoping against hope he would get tired and somehow fall asleep, I left him in his room. I didn't know what else to do. I trudged wearily downstairs with that word, "why?" ringing in my head.

I know more now than I did then. I know now that part of the reason my son wouldn't obey me was my un-Christlike spirit. Christ was not in control of my life; I was. Matthew was only reflecting back to me my own anger and frustrations. I didn't understand that to gain heartfelt, inwardly motivated obedience required me to win his heart for Jesus.

As I sat in my chair, mulling things over, I kept hearing a little voice prompting me, "*Win the heart.*"

"What does that mean?" I wondered.

Jesus reminded me of the Bible verse, "My son, give me thine heart" (Proverbs 23:26). I thought about it, trying to correlate the idea to something I understood. I began to understand that winning the heart must be at the core of raising my children for Christ. I knew if Jesus had their heart, miracles would happen. Hearts would change, and true obedience would be the result. So I began thinking about the heart. What was there about the human heart that God wanted me to understand?

Physically, the heart is just a pump circulating the lifeblood throughout the body. I was a nurse, and I remembered some of my patients whose hearts had been terribly damaged by poor lifestyle or by disease. No matter their condition, however, their hearts didn't refuse to pump their blood. The heart doesn't discriminate between good blood or bad; it just pumps what is there! With good blood, the heart pumps a joyful, healthy life. I thought of this as representing Christ's life and character flowing through me to be acted out in kind words and deeds. With bad blood, the same heart pumps a bitter, diseased, life. This represents Satan's life and character flowing through my life and bringing the diseases of a defective character. The Bible says that as a person "thinketh in his heart, so is he" (Proverbs 23:7). Spiritually, the heart represents my thoughts, so my mind must be a "thought pump." The heart God wants is our thoughts and feelings.

With this realization came a more sobering idea. What if the thought pump works just like the heart and pumps whatever we have placed there, good or bad? My thoughts circulate, bringing either life or death. And then the idea struck home as I realized that those same thoughts can easily be transferred to my children. What thoughts am I giving my child to pump through his or her system today—and to what effect? If I don't filter my thoughts through Christ before I express them, I can be used by Satan to reproduce his character traits in my child. Matthew didn't have Christ's character when I tried to put him down for a nap, but how did he get that way? Through me! He just reflected what I provided him physically, mentally, and spiritually.

"Lord, so this is why You call so often for my heart. You are trying to teach me how to give all the wrong thoughts to You in exchange for Your good thoughts so that I can pass them on to my children. You want to use me to win my child's heart so that he can have Your power to obey and to do what I ask as his parent. And You can't use me to do that unless I am experiencing this same process."

Life has taught me that if I hear or say something often enough, I believe it. It matters not whether it is right or wrong. Now apply this principle in our homes. If I think my child is naughty, my thoughts are reflected in my feelings, and I treat him coldly. I'll be uninterested, curt, or critical, not because I set out to be that way, but because my thoughts alter my behavior or response, and my child will get the message whether I convey it in words or body language. If he gets these negative messages repeatedly, he will think of himself as naughty even if he isn't. I can predispose my child to think of himself as bad, and the thoughts I place in his thought pump will bring about fruit in the form of bad behavior because as he thinks, so he becomes. We parents have the greatest influence in our children's lives. We must realize that they are what we, not someone else, have made them.

Now if I let God change *my* thoughts, if I think and dwell on the thought that through Christ my child can be good, my actions, thoughts, and responses will be aimed at encouraging this. I will tell my child over and over what he can be in Jesus. I will take the role and attitude of a helper to my child, rather than the role of judge, jury, and executor of the sentence.

What we think is often why we react the way we do. When we think how irritating our child's behavior is, how do we react to him? Generally, in an irritated manner! When we are thinking fretful, faultfinding thoughts about our children, how will we respond to them? In a fretful, faultfinding manner, of course. When we are frustrated, for whatever reason, how do we react when crossing wills with our children? Frustrating thoughts flow into our emotions, and we respond to our children in a frustrated, angry way, even if they are not the cause of our anger. This is the voice of the flesh or Satan.

When we are thinking about our child's good behavior, how do we react to him then? I know I usually respond with kind words, pleased smiles, and an encouraging spirit. When we think grateful thoughts about our child's helpfulness, how do we react? When we identify our child's weaknesses only to help him or her to overcome it, when we prayerfully plan to cultivate the opposite trait in him or her through a connection with God, how do we react? As we cooperate with these good thoughts, we are obeying *the voice of God,* and sweetness flows through our thought pump.

Whoever gets the thoughts gets the heart—the feelings, emotions, habits, inclinations, desires—in short the whole of our being. Both God and Satan strive for this dominant position at the head of our thoughts—and those of our children.

God plants in the heart of every child a desire to please his parents and hence God, whom the parent represents. Our job is to make this option appealing. Are we giving the child a pattern worthy of imitation, which will plant hope in his heart that he *can* control his thoughts? Our children need to know a personal Savior, and they need to see that we know the Savior before they are able to imitate a good pattern. My thoughts create in my child attitudes and feelings that form his character. If my thoughts are wrong, everything else will be wrong.

All of us need to feel loved and lovingly labored with when we have a fault. Why is it that we act as if this were not true for our children? If they feel we've given up on them, they will give up on themselves. If they feel we haven't given up on them, neither will they. If we are wonderful, helpful, and encouraging, we demonstrate Christ to them as He truly is, and they will be less likely to shun God. This requires that we understand in practical terms the concept of the thought pump and God having the heart. Leading our child to choose right thoughts and right feelings in Jesus is the foundation to all successful parenting practices. Without Christ in us, we cannot battle successfully against the lying thoughts or perverted emotions that Satan stirs up.

One day when Matthew was very young, I took him shopping with me. For a two-year-old child, a store is a place of wonder.

"Mommy! Mommy! I want!" He shouted, pointing an excited finger. He stood up in the shopping cart, almost bouncing with excitement.

"Matthew, stop it! Just be quiet and sit down, so I can get my list done!"

"Mommy! Mommy! I—"

"No! Stop bothering me!"

"Mommy, buy me—"

I tried to tune him out and get my work done. As I headed down another aisle, Matthew reached out and snatched a package that was close enough for him to pull into the cart. He sat down to savor his accomplishment. Mom might not know what to do in the store, but he was going to have some fun!

"Matthew, what are you doing?" I demanded, as if it weren't obvious. "You know you shouldn't do that!" I took away his treasure. "Stop being such a bother!" I said with finality.

He looked at me like "What's the matter with Mother?"

"Can I have—?" he said, starting to rise.

"No! Now sit down and be quiet." I shoved him down in the cart. "I don't want to hear another word out of you."

His little head dropped, and he pouted quietly in the cart. I finished my shopping in relative peace and quiet. I had gained outward compliance with my harsh correction, but I didn't have his heart. I was content that he had complied with my desires. I didn't consider the results of my behavior on his thinking and attitude. But I soon found out. As I was putting him into his car seat, his selfishness exploded. He cried, pushing away from me and refusing to let me buckle him in. I didn't know what to do. He was doing everything he could to get away from me. I had wounded his spirit, and he was offended.

"Matthew, stop this and let me put you in your car seat! You need to quiet down." He fought all the harder. My thoughts were desperate. "Lord, I'm so tired. I'm up all night with Andrew and all day with Matthew. After two months, I'm exhausted! What do I do with this child? I can't get him to obey."

"Would you like Me to help you?" This was not an audible voice, but rather a thought in my head. I was talking to God, but I wasn't really expecting an answer.

My need prompted me to quickly respond, "Yes."

Then Jesus said, *"Put Matthew in My hands."*

"Okay Lord, You may have him—his mind, his heart, his will—everything is Yours."

"Tell Matthew he can't behave this way; he must choose to do right, trusting in Jesus."

"Haven't I been doing that?"

"Yes. But you've been doing so in harshness and anger. That won't work. Tell him in a loving way."

"You mean I can tell him 'No' in a loving way?" I was so distraught I argued with God. "That won't work, he's all upset. I've been through this before; no reasoning will do any good here. This is so embarrassing in the parking lot. What if someone sees me wrestling with my child like this?"

"Sally, trust Me! I'm your Helper in trouble. First, give Me your heart."

"Okay, I'll try." First I gave God my emotions, feelings, and fears—and oh, yes, my thoughts.

Then I said with love, "Matthew you may not behave this way. Trusting Jesus, you must choose to do right and let me buckle you into your car seat."

He didn't settle down one bit. He pushed and shoved against me still, trying to get down. "Lord, what should I do?" (See Acts 9:6.) I was quickly daunted because the first effort didn't work.

"Tell him that he has chosen a spanking for disobeying." The Lord was calm, but firm.

"But, Lord, that won't work! It inflames him when he is like this. I've done this many times, and was I ever sorry I did! Besides, what if someone sees me spanking my child? Is spanking ever good or just an admission of failure?"

"I'm not against spanking in the right spirit. Didn't I spank Israel, so to speak, for disobedience? Their punishment was a motivation to choose right and discover My redeeming grace. Giving a spanking without harshness and anger—surrendered to Me—will be different than when you did it on your own. Why don't you at least try?"

"Lord, today, they can take your child away if you spank him in public."

"Yes, Satan is against spanking because it restrains the child from his service. But remember, most people understand only the wrong type of spanking, the kind that vents an adult's anger and frustration. Of course, this kind of spanking is not redemptive, but Satan hopes to use this false image to sweep away all childhood restraint. Are you going to let the fear of man keep you from trusting Me?"

I struggled with these thoughts while I was physically restraining my squirming son. Deciding at last, I followed through as best I knew how, spanking without harshness or anger. Then I said to Matthew, "You must give your selfishness to Jesus, and He will change your heart and feelings."

I was expecting World War III at this point, but instead Matthew looked up at me. Seeing love in my eyes, he settled down and stopped fighting. We had a simple prayer. "Now let me buckle you in your car seat." He calmly let me buckle him in. All the wrestling, fighting, and crying were gone! I looked at my son in awe! Never had I seen such a miraculous transformation in his disposition! The fight just drained right out of him before my eyes. Then he smiled at me.

As I got into the car and started the drive home, I kept looking into my rearview mirror to see if this miracle was real. It was! "What did I do right?" I thought. "Whatever it was, I want to do it again!"

I had simply responded to the voice of God offering me help. I surrendered to God's thought, chose to do it, and then I did it, remaining in the Spirit, trusting Jesus would work the miracle on my heart and hopefully my son's. While I did all I knew to do, at the same time I was asking God to temper my son's disposition and make him mild and gentle. Why should it surprise me that God answered my prayer?

A child's expression tells the parent what the inner thoughts are. He or she may outwardly yield to our forcible control, but this does not unlock the heart. Indeed it locks it up. Many parents label their children as strong-willed, selfish, or rebellious, and they may indeed be, but often the reality is that the parents' wrong thoughts, words, and actions are the origin of their misbehavior. What we sow, we reap (see Job 4:8). The seed determines the harvest, and when we choose to let God control our thoughts and have our heart, we free His hands to communicate understanding to our children and change their disposition with His divine power. If our children see us choosing to obey, they will be encouraged to make the same free-will choice. This is your key to success. Divine power does not replace human effort. Both are essential, but divine power dethrones selfishness when we unite with Christ.

The Bible says of the thought pump—the heart—"A merry heart doeth good like a medicine: but a broken spirit drieth the bones" (Proverbs 17:22). When we think good thoughts, the heart pumps healing to our system. When we think negative thoughts, it dries up our bones. Parents have the greatest influence on their child's thought life—either for good or evil.

So how do I think loving thoughts and express love to my family, especially when correction is needed? I began learning with my foot in a cast. God used my slower pace as the perfect opportunity to teach me a valuable lesson. My boys were playing on the floor in front of me as I rested with my foot on a chair when they began to fuss for possession of a toy. As I began to sit up to scold them, my thoughts were interrupted.

"Sally, study their dispositions."

I sensed God was trying to teach me something, but my reason was rebelling against God's call. "Study their dispositions? That's ridiculous

Lord! What do You want me to do—let them fight it out before me and say nothing?"

"Sally, study their dispositions."

"Study their dispositions? What is the disposition anyway? Isn't it just thoughts, feelings, and the way we naturally react?" I looked into Matthew's eyes and began to understand what God wanted me to do. God didn't want me just to stop the outward battles; He wanted me to understand *why* they responded the way they did. God wasn't as concerned with their outward behavior as He was that I see the bigger picture of getting inside their minds. Realizing this, I started my analysis. "Matthew is not mad," I told myself. "He's trying to convince his brother that this toy is rightfully his. He wants that toy. He's being kind, but dominant. Andrew is upset. He's trying hard physically to obtain the toy, but his tugging is useless because his brother is stronger. I've seen this before. He knows his brother usually wins. Oh, see that look now. He's given up, and he looks so sad. I wonder why? I see, it's not the toy so much; he is sad because he thinks he can't win and that life is miserable. He let his brother have it and went away to be sad by himself—the poor kid!"

Now I saw the importance of understanding their dispositions. I started to decide what actions were needed. Matthew needed to ask and give in sometimes—not always try to dominate. He needed to learn to put his brother first. The leader must practice being the servant to balance his strong personality. I would have to let him see life from his brother's side. Right thoughts would influence right responses.

My personality made me much more attuned to Andrew's problem of thinking that he couldn't be as good as his brother and giving up on himself. I couldn't *tell* him he was good; I had to build him up to *see* that God loved him—that I loved him—and that he could do well with Jesus and be content with who he is. Andrew needed to learn to toughen up and not be so easily daunted. It might require strong correction to overcome the effect of the lying thoughts he held. The truth and God needed to become more real to him than the lies of Satan. I also needed to show him some better problem-solving techniques than just giving up. Instead of letting Andrew give up, I had to nurture perseverance. I had to show Matthew how to be more tender. The boys and I talked right then and there, and I had them reenact the former scene with better problem-solving techniques. It was a good beginning.

On another occasion, my friend Crystal and I sat at the table visiting after lunch. Just then her sweet, playful son, Jesse, raced in looking for something fun to do. Spotting a fork, and making sure Mother saw him so that they could play chase, he grabbed it and ran giggling for the living room. "That sunken living room!" Crystal exclaimed, "He'll fall for sure! Stop!" And she leaped up to run after him.

Catching the laughing youngster, she deftly removed the fork and placed him across her knee, spanking him with all the frustration and anger that his action had caused her. "You terrible child," she said after placing him upright. "Don't you ever do that again! Go off and play now!"

Her thoughts and feelings drove her, and she obeyed them. What was she placing into her child's thought pump? Why fear, of course! He didn't understand why he deserved such severe punishment. He was only being playful; he didn't sense the danger of his actions. He felt very wrongly treated. Put yourself in his shoes. When the spirit of the parent is unfair, when you are scolded and hit in anger, it wounds you to the core—especially when you are treated that way by the person you love the most and depend upon totally.

I watched this child's eyes, and I could see this reaction. He backed up, distancing himself from her with fear in his eyes and confusion. His mother had placed fear in his thought pump; she told him he was bad. His sense of justice told him he was treated unfairly. Satan never misses such an opportunity to suggest lying thoughts to a child's mind. "Mother doesn't love you." The next time mother's expression is angry, the lying thought is confirmed in his mind, "Mother doesn't love me." It's not true, but the child knows only how you were with him before. The negative perception of himself is deepened and confirmed; it makes no difference if it is based in reality or not.

Let's revisit Crystal in the same situation—except this time she has been re-trained to remain under Christ's control instead of reacting automatically without thinking.

When Jesse grabs the fork to play chase, her first reaction is still fear for his safety and a desire is to save him from himself. But this time she pauses just a moment and the blessed delay brings this thought, *"Don't chase him; work this through calmly. I'm with you."*

She walks slowly and calls cheerfully to her child, choosing to follow Christ's leading. Her focus now is on understanding why he grabbed the fork, rather than alarm over the danger.

"Jesse it's not safe to run with the fork; you can hurt yourself. Give Mother the fork."

Jesse still wants to play "keep away." His idea has almost worked; he *does* have Mother's attention. So he responds playfully with a come-and-get-it attitude.

Still asking God, "What should I do now?" Crystal feels impressed to sit down and call Jesse to her. The idea came from God, yet the results are beyond her wisdom. She has just sent a strong nonverbal message—she will not play chase with the fork. At the same time she has become less threatening by getting down on his level. Her request, given in a polite, cheerful tone, affirms to him the importance she places upon him. He still wants to play, but Mother is offering him her attention—her lap even—and that is just too good an offer to pass by. He makes his way to her lap, still holding the fork. Crystal makes no attempt to take it from him, wanting a free-will decision—not a forced one.

"Did you want to play with Mother?" she asks.

"Yes," he nods, "I want to play."

"I love playing with you! I like to play chase, too, but playing chase with a fork is too dangerous. Give me the fork, and we will go get a ball and play chase with that." He willingly surrenders the fork. In obeying his mother, he finds the desires of his heart are granted. Mother made obedience sweet, and he willingly chose it. Crystal keeps her word and plays. Even if her child had become stubborn and refused to give up the fork, it would have been better to punish, even spank, him while he held the fork than to grab it from his hand.

You can see the contrast of the two ways of parenting. Does this mean there is never a time to act fast to prevent injury? Of course not. God gave you a mind to reason with, and He expects you will use it wisely. Especially will you need wisdom in dealing with special-needs children who have to struggle not just with inclinations to do evil but with malfunctioning minds sometimes coupled with physical disorders. Help them be the best they can be in Jesus. Teach and train and labor with them to hear the voice of God as well. God is able to communicate with them in a way that is beyond human wisdom or ability. God will surely be with you because of your need. These children carry terrible damage already. You want them to be as disciplined and self-controlled as they can be in Jesus. Treat them according to their ability and understanding, but don't leave out Christ. All parents need to be firm, consistent, loving, and willing to give appropriate consequences to help their children learn. Never discipline in harshness and anger.

When you have never yielded to God and finally learn how to surrender, you think you have found the secret to the Christian walk. But before long you find out that another step is involved—the art of cooperation. Cooperation connects you to Christ, your source of power; it's the factor that makes your choices a reality and gives you the divine power to carry through on the choices made.

Right by the counter was a rack filled to overflowing with the most luscious gum, and best of all, it was free for the taking because Grandma was treating! Andrew, age three, didn't find all aspects of shopping exciting, but this was a special thrill. He always dug through the whole rack, making sure he picked the two very best pieces—one for him and one for his brother. It had become a part of shopping when Grandma and I went out, and Andrew looked forward to it.

The problem was that we had decided the boys didn't benefit from the sugar and had decided not to buy gum any more. So I had to say, "Mother, we've decided that we wouldn't buy any more bubble gum."

"What's the matter with bubble gum?" she asked.

"It's because of the sugar, their teeth, and their health."

"Can't you let it go this once?" my mother pled, seeing Andrew already had the gum in his hands.

"No, he needs to put it back. I'm sorry I didn't tell you ahead of time, Mother. Letting it go will just make things harder the next time."

Andrew was so sweet. He struggled to obey. He held his chubby little hand above the rack, looking up at me with pleading eyes, hoping I'd relent just this time so that he wouldn't have to put it back.

"Mama, I want some bubble gum." he said sweetly. I hated to do it, but I shook my head "No." As he put the gum back, he put his finger in his mouth, and the tears began to roll down his cheeks. It broke my heart.

Matthew said, "Can't we have it just one more time?"

"No," I said with more conviction than I felt.

Everyone was so quiet as we walked to the car. My mother was very sad. She doesn't agree with us, but bless her heart, she's always been supportive of what we have decided to do; she doesn't go against our wishes even when it goes against her heart and reason.

As we were driving, Andrew slipped out of his car seat to kneel on the floor just behind my mother's seat. He began to pray earnestly out loud to God in this great trial. "Oh, dear Jesus, I want bubble gum! Help me not want bubble gum. Mama says I can't have bubble gum, but I want bubble gum. Oh, dear Jesus I want to obey Mama. I want my bubble gum! I want to obey Mama! I want my bubble gum!"

And so the struggle went. Andrew was sobbing as he prayed. We all witnessed his agony. Matthew is crying for his brother and himself. My mother is crying silently in the seat next to me, trying to stay out of it. I'm cut to the heart, with tears running down my cheeks. I don't know how to help my son out of this!

"Andrew, dear," I put my hand on his back, comforting him as best I could. "You need to get back into your car seat now. It will be alright, honey."

He returned to his car seat, but continued to cry for a long time. He was still sad and disappointed that evening. Nothing brought relief—except time.

Why is doing right so very hard? I had given Andrew experience in prayer and surrender. Like so many Christians, he knew what was right and wanted to obey, but his only source of power was to grit his teeth and force his unwilling flesh to obey his choice. Instinctively he knew that God was the solution. He prayed. However, at that time I didn't know myself how God removes feeling we don't want. So I was powerless to guide him through the experience of choosing to do what is right *in Jesus' power.*

Andrew's dilemma is like an eagle exercising only one of its two wings, and this is why he could not rise above the pull of his flesh and get above his desire for the bubble gum. Exercising only the wing of surrender sends you in a circle. The second wing—cooperation—is vital for true flight above the pull of our flesh. Andrew needed to cry out to God *and* do whatever God told him to do. This is being "in Christ." In this way, God enters us to do battle in His divine power against sin and self by recreating our thoughts, feelings, and desires. God works from the inside out, not only with our surrender—the mental assent that He is right—but, vitally, in the cooperation of our will. God will not force us against our will. Without the exercise of this second "wing," we are not redeemed and find that we are powerless to change of ourselves.

For Andrew that would have meant putting forth the same strong effort he was making to do right, but it would also involve surrendering repeatedly and giving those desires to Jesus. Then as he cooperated with Jesus-led right thoughts to replace the desire for gum, he would have found victory. Gum was not the enemy; thoughts were. But I didn't understand this back then.

Today, I would use the "replacement principle" for Andrew's desired bubble gum. He needed to choose to be happy with an apple, or some juice, and ask God to perform this miracle to bring contentment inside him (see Hebrews 13:5). This could have made the exchange physically tangible for Andrew. When it is only abstract, it's hard for our little ones to understand the spiritual battle we are involved in.

How many of our children grow up sincerely trying to obey, honestly trying to be good and do what is right—but have Andrew's experience as he prayed in the back seat of the car, struggling against self and the flesh, with no notable victory or relief? Their parents may know *about* God, but because they don't know God *personally,* they cannot tell their children how to have victory. We must come to know how to set our children free from the flesh by connecting with God. If they gain this experience, we will have living, vibrant, courageous youth.

It is so sad how many youth I talk with that have a downcast view of Christianity. The majority wants nothing to do with the religion they know. Why? Because Andrew's struggle has been theirs—and their parent's—year after year after year, until at last they give up on religion, their church, their parents, and sometimes on themselves. These youth had bubble gum desires but never found the power to overcome them. We have given them a crippled religion and a powerless god to worship. One teen expressed it this way: "This religion stuff may work for others, but I've tried and tried, and it doesn't work for me. There must be something wrong with me. God doesn't answer my prayers. My dad is a loser, and I'm just like him. They all tell me so. There is no hope for me. So I gave up trying to be kind and nice. I might burn one day, but there is nothing I can do about it."

Is it any wonder they follow these lying thoughts of Satan's when they find no personal God and no power to make their choices real? They don't know how to connect and cooperate with God to gain His power. Our children deserve the heritage of a personal God and an empowered life. To a large degree, our actions as parents will determine whether they enter adulthood as children of the heavenly kingdom or subjects of the kingdom of darkness.

If you would like to transform your thoughts and hence your child's, you will need to surrender your choices before the wisdom of an all-knowing God. And as you do so, you will see great transformations of character and attitude no matter what the age of your child. You can be the key to unlocking the treasures of heaven's blessing upon your family.

Is it worth the effort? If you could but see one transformation, you would say it was worth all it costs and more. Our heavenly Father will pour His thoughts into you, if you are willing. When we stand together on heaven's shore, don't be too shocked if we realize then that it was through our hearts—our thought pumps—that we were most transformed and received the greatest benefits. Praise God that He has provided a way for us to be free from the power of wrong thoughts!

THE LONE EMBRACE
A SPECIAL WORD OF ENCOURAGEMENT FOR SINGLE PARENTS

Of all the things that I have shared in my counseling over the years, this understanding of the way in which our thoughts affect our children's thoughts just might be one of the most beneficial to the single parent. The reason is that so many single parents carry resentments, anger, and guilt over the situation in which they find themselves. They hope and pray they can keep from making their children bitter or angry, but don't understand that such is almost certainly going to be the case unless their hearts—their thought pumps—are transformed.

The situation you face is hard, but you also have a blessed opportunity that someone in a two-parent household cannot experience. You alone have the greatest input into the child's thought pump; no other influence can rival your own. If the ideas you install are of heavenly origin, the thoughts will lead upward. My prayer is that you will take the necessary steps for your mind to provide your child with a pure flow of heavenly thoughts.

Chapter 9

DOES YOUR SCHEDULE
MATCH YOUR PRIORITIES?

"To every thing there is a season, and a time to every purpose under the heaven" (Ecclesiastes 3:1).

*W*e were halfway around the world at Sadie's invitation to come and share our messages. Arriving at her home where we were staying the week, several things struck me, but none so much as Sadie herself. This woman was a single mom who ran an active ministry out of her home. She was energetic and enthusiastic, but almost immediately, I felt something was seriously wrong.

The house was not neat or clean. Mealtimes were late and irregular. I thought maybe Sadie was just overwhelmed; I offered to help, but when I inspected the kitchen, I quickly found that not enough food was on hand to cook a decent meal. It wasn't that Sadie couldn't afford a variety of foods. The problem was that, for her, food for herself and her family didn't seem important in light of the great work she was doing for God. So her family ate whatever she could throw together.

Unless someone was supervising her children at every step, they would slip away, leaving their assigned tasks undone. They couldn't endure the smallest correction. They were the worst-behaved children in the church. They lay in the aisles during services, and no one corrected them. Their mother was in the pulpit, explaining how successful she was in her work and how hard her children worked in the home. I wondered how she could be so deceived. By any objective view, her children's condition would raise questions about her ministry and her use of time. It seemed impossible that she didn't realize her home was not what she was making it out to be.

Introspection isn't a bad thing, and neither is an honest assessment of our true condition. You can be sure God was trying to open Sadie's eyes, but her schedule was too rushed for God to have an opportunity to show her the truth about herself. She repeatedly claimed her children were the most important thing in her life. Yet where did she spend her time? She was consumed in ministry for others, while the mission field of her home remained uncultivated, leaving her own heritage to become seriously damaged—all in the name of doing the Lord's work! Her lack of involvement with her children provided Satan the opportunity to sow the seeds of his character in their hearts, and I can testify that Satan's garden was growing just fine! Her lack of honesty was her downfall. Her too-busy schedule crowded out God's leading. She thought she was ministering to others, when in reality she was leaving the Lord's real work undone! Did her schedule match her stated priority? What will God say to her one day? More importantly, what will God say to you and me one day? Do our schedules match our priorities?

There was a time when I, too, would have said, "I love my children above everything," while my actual time use said just the opposite. You see, I found the schedule I lived didn't match my priorities. I've talked to many women who feel as I did—that their relationship with the Lord is floundering, that they are falling far short of the important work that needs to be done for their own salvation and the saving of their families. Again and again, they have tried to get control of their schedules, but it never quite works. Then the helpless feeling of being out of control drags them toward despair. My observations and conversations with literally hundreds of women demonstrate that the problem we find most difficult is that of following God in the scheduling of our homes. I remember praying about my schedule, knowing I needed to change and knowing as well that I had no idea how to do so! The Lord kindly enlightened me on a few things, and I'd like to share them with you.

"Sally, you are looking too much to yourself to accomplish changes. That is what brings you to hopelessness. Look to My strength and just be a sheep that follows Me," the Lord coached me tenderly.

"I have so much to change, Lord. How can I change that much? It's hopeless!"

"Sally, one step at a time takes you on a far journey. You are trying to make that journey in one giant step, and you can't, no matter how much or how hard you try. Look at the hands on your clock. In your eagerness, you are like the little hand resting on the twelve, and you see yourself in need of being on the six. Time has a sequence it must go through, and the Christian walk, too, has a sequence you must go through to reach successful change. The clock moves in its steady path one click at a time. So, too, with the changes in your schedule. One change, one choice, at a time incorporated into your home—and then kept one click at a time—will one day bring your hand to the six, as you desire."

One item prayerfully focused on and mastered, before moving on to other items, is the key to change, and we are most likely to start this process with the activities that make up what I call the "skeleton schedule." As our physical skeleton supports our body and protects its internal organs, so too, a "skeleton schedule" supports the home life by its consistency. It gives structure and protects those inside it from circumstances crowding out physical and spiritual essentials.

Our schedule is as follows—not for you to copy, but as a pattern. Our schedule and yours will vary. That's okay.

The Hohnberger Schedule
5:30 A.M. - Personal prayer, study and worship
8:00 A.M. - Family worship (generally an interesting 20 minutes)
8:30 A.M. - Breakfast
3:00 P.M. - Supper
6:30 P.M. - Family fun time
8:00 P.M. - Family worship
8:30 P.M. - Bedtime

As you begin making changes, pick one item to start with. Let's say you choose a workable time for you to retire at night. Now apply yourself to make the changes necessary to go to bed at that time every night. You'll be surprised at how hard it is to keep even one item on a schedule consistently! The only true means to success is to rely upon God and reach out to Him for strength. The logic of your scheduling plan and your decisive choice to stick with it must overrule feelings and emotions that you can be sure will war against this sudden new restraint.

In reality, every schedule begins the night before. If you don't go to bed on time, you can't worship God as you desire the next day because your mind will be too tired to worship. You'll likely spend your time dozing, or at best be crippled by exhaustion in your worship. You will make or break your schedule by what time you go to bed. Consistency and staying in touch with God are the two secrets to lasting success.

The human body demonstrates to us that we are creatures designed by God to respond best to regularity and schedules. When we eat meals at regularly scheduled times, our bodies are dependable, preparing themselves for a meal by making digestive juices. It takes teamwork to bring all this to pass properly. God made our bodies to be timely. They love regularity in every aspect of life. So, too, when we worship at a set time, our minds actually prepare, in attitude and disposition, and we can better assimilate our spiritual food.

Any schedule you create will always have kinks. Let's look at how the Lord helped me work through one of mine. I had a hard time getting breakfast on the table when it was supposed to be. Now, ten minutes late may not seem like much, but it left me feeling rushed and pressured, which in turn left me far more likely to be impatient with my children and started us all into our day running a few minutes behind. "Lord, I am typically behind in my breakfast time. Please help me be timely." The very next morning, during my personal worship time, the thought came into my mind, *"Sally, what about breakfast?"*

"Breakfast?" I said to myself. "Oh I have at least ten or fifteen minutes before I have to get breakfast." I picked my book back up. Fifteen minutes later, I dashed to put my book away and ran to the kitchen to prepare breakfast. It was a rush job, and breakfast was ten minutes late again—as usual.

I had asked God for help being timely, and I found myself asking, "Where was my help, Lord?"

"I did help Sally. I reminded you of the time, and you ignored Me."

"Oh dear, will I ever learn? Well, what do I do next time?"

"You don't need to fret or despair. Just learn from this to make the necessary adjustments for tomorrow."

I love this about God. He never holds today's failures against us; He only builds with us for a better future. So I thought about the situation, and it didn't take very long to realize that I was allowing just the minimum amount of time to make breakfast and that in the real world things rarely go that smoothly. "Lord, I'm consistently ten minutes late because I begin ten minutes too late. I'll plan differently!"

The next morning I made waffles. Instead of starting just in time, I decided to make up the batter and then study while the waffles cooked, stopping now and then to take a finished one out and pour another. I was done early! I was relaxed and happy. It was amazing how much happier the whole family was because I didn't feel rushed! I was so pleased that I continued learning how to allow sufficient time for meal preparation, and bit by bit, timely meals became my new pattern.

Order is the first law of the universe. Every creature from the tiniest element to the greatest solar system follows rules of order and discipline. If you lack order, don't worry, God can create order in you, when you believe and cooperate with Him. If you don't know how to be timely, God can show you. Are you weary and weak? Look to His strength. Are you disorganized? Ask Him to teach you order and organization. Do you lack ideas of how to change? Come to the "idea God" of love. "If any of you lack wisdom, let him ask of God, that giveth to all men liberally, . . . and it shall be given him" (James 1:5). God will do as He says!

Getting organized deals with the roots of selfishness. It calls for the dethroning of self. This is real heart work. I must step down from being the one in charge and submit, instead, to God's control. Logic must rule over my feelings and old habits.

After you have built in your skeleton schedule of essentials and have it working well, you can start fleshing it out. This process will take a different route with each person. Some can take more than one step at a time, while others can manage only one. What matters is that you succeed, and I caution you to avoid the discouragement of attempting too large a change at one time. Some have bitten off so much change that it's like attempting to eat an entire elephant at one sitting. We need to learn how to eat an elephant one bite at a time under God's direction.

Fleshing out the schedule is the stage where all the nuts and bolts that make up the minutes of life find a home on our skeleton schedule. It requires you to plan carefully, on paper, each thing that needs to be done in the day. Make a list. Then refine the list, making sure nothing has been overlooked. It's very discouraging to do all this work of planning a schedule, only to overlook some important task and have to start over. The old carpenter's rule—measure twice and cut once—applies here.

After you are certain of your needs, take your skeleton schedule and find a good time for each item to happen. Make sure every set of hands has a part to play, no matter how small. Even the very youngest can gain the joy of helping. Teamwork is fun, so divide up the labor. Mother is not to be the slave. You hurt your children when you do all the work, and they do all the play. It also makes them very selfish. We need to work together in a loving spirit. We want our children to love to be with us, working side by side together.

My fleshed out *morning* schedule at that time looked like this:

5:30 A.M.   Mother rises—personal care, start cookstove
6:00 A.M.   Mother's prayer and study time
            Boys rise—personal care
6:30 A.M.   Mother oversees boys' personal worship
7:30 A.M.   Mother or responsible child—prepare meal
            Boys—house chores: sweep, empty trash, start laundry, make beds

8:00 A.M.   Family worship

8:30 A.M.   Breakfast

9:30 A.M.   All—Kitchen clean up and other chores:

10:00 A.M. School subject

11:00 A.M. School subject

12:00 P.M. 15 min break—prayer and story

12:15 P.M. Boys—physical work for home, gardening, yard

Parents—swing time

Here's what I did in each of these time frames—and some tips I learned as I went along:

5:30 A.M.-7:30 A.M. Starting the wood cookstove was an essential element for our home. We had no fire or heat in the house all night, and although the logs radiated retained heat, it was about sixty degrees in the early morning, and we all wanted the heat of our cookstove. Little tasks like this must find a place on the schedule or they will end up robbing time from other areas.

My schedule was influenced by our having one bathroom. Jim and I would rise and have bathroom time, and then the boys had their time. I allotted fifteen minutes per person, and it worked very well for us. Teaching the boys how to have personal prayer in their own private spot and then self-directed Bible studies at the kitchen table was a challenge, but it laid the foundation for good habits.

7:30 A.M.-8:00 A.M. In the beginning years, I did the meal preparation with some help from my boys, but it was predominately my job. We divided up all the other household chores amongst the four of us. Andrew was in charge of emptying all the trash from the wastebaskets, sweeping the front and back porches, and cleaning up the bathroom. Matthew was in charge of making our beds, vacuuming, and getting the laundry sorted and going.

These chores were done every day to build a habit. The porches didn't need sweeping every day, nor did the carpet need vacuuming, but the boys needed the consistency of forming habits. Later when the

5—P.B.T.S.

habits were well established and more mature judgment developed, these two duties were done only as needed.

The responsible person did his chore list for one month. Then we swapped the chore lists around for the next month until lists were no longer needed because we knew them by memory. Once the routine was well established, all of us would sometimes pick up an undone task for another just to surprise them with a gift of love. Once habits are established, everything functions like clockwork! I've had visitors say that everything important seemed to just get done automatically in our home. They ask, "What's your secret, Sally?" The secret is a consistent schedule coupled with habits of service and dependable teamwork.

8:00 A.M. Family worship is a very special time of day. Make your worship time interesting. Long prayers, dull lessons, or just reading will lose the attention and interest of your children and youth. We've found that taking turns with the reading is very helpful to keep their attention. We ask the reader to summarize what he or she has read. Sharing and discussion helps make it personal for everyone and is another valuable tool in learning, retaining, and maintaining interest. Experiment!

Our schedules will reflect our priorities. Time with God is my focus to begin my day. If this gets crowded out, who is running the show? If we leave Christ out, then I can guarantee you that Satan takes His place and works his will and way. He wants his evil character traits to have sway in my character. Do your priorities match your schedule?

8:30 A.M. Make breakfast a desirable social time with the family at the table. You can carry over some points of interest from family worship and continue the conversation around the breakfast table. Make your conversation as positive as you know. It is the parents that make the home atmosphere attractive as Christ is—or unattractive. I have allotted an hour for breakfast. This is one area I allow some flexibility. If a phone call comes that needs to be taken care of, this gives me space not to feel rushed. If a conflict comes up regarding my child's will, I have time for dealing with it without undue pressure. If a conversation that is very beneficial comes up at breakfast, we can complete it, for this is *always* good use of my time. Or the boys could start school early and gain extra time for their personal use later. They liked that, and I found it cultivated the lovely trait of self-government in my boys.

9:30 A.M. Clean up should be a lovely social time for the family. You can sing, enjoy good conversation, or simply discuss your special focus for the day. You can race to clean up, making work fun, and if you vary your approaches, you'll find even more joy. One son would clear the table, put away all the food, sweep the kitchen floor, and vacuum the living room if necessary. The second son would wash, dry, and put away the dishes. When this was completed, the laundry would be finished, so whoever was free helped hang or fold and put away, while the ironing was stacked for later. At this point of the day, everything was clean and tidy, and the house was perfectly presentable.

10:00 A.M. School starts for us. I allotted one hour for each subject, and I began with the hardest subject for my boys. They have the greatest energy at the beginning of the day, so that is when we should face the hardest task. For my boys, that was English. If they applied themselves and got their work done efficiently and well, they could have the time remaining for a walk, a bike ride, or to read a book of their choice. Again, I found that this kindled self-government in a very positive way. It was a self-rewarding system. If they chose, they could also use the extra time to do an extra lesson in this subject to get ahead so that they could take time off for a special outing another day.

After instructing them in their studies, I'd make bread, iron, write letters, or do other jobs. When they finished their lesson, I'd promptly examine it and return it to them to correct. So the class was conducted, and the lesson was done and corrected within that hour. That meant *no* homework!

11:00 A.M. Another subject for school is done in similar fashion.

12:00 noon. After a number of years, we added a fifteen-minute break in the school program at noon. It was nice to have prayer and a short story just to reconnect with God. We all tend to wander away so easily. I didn't think that we had time for this but found that it was a good addition, and our time didn't seem hindered. Let God lead you in making changes in your schedule. He wants to be your Principal and you the underteacher—not only if you home school but for all parents who are developing the character of Christ in their children. We need a power outside of ourselves to direct us.

12:15 P.M. I found that, for my boys, a balance of mental and physical work was very helpful and lessened a lot of problems that occurred if I kept them on scholastics only. The mind grows weary, and a little physical or outside work worked wonders on attitude and ability. Shoveling snow in the winter, raking in the spring, mowing the lawn, taking care of the garden and the greenhouse in the summer, or any household cleaning tasks provided many options to maintain this balance.

While the boys worked, Jim and I had our swing time—a special time for the husband and wife to visit and reconnect.

Your schedule won't be perfect overnight. You may find that circumstances are controlling your life and that you need to consider prayerfully the necessary changes. Change requires effort, thought, planning, and then executing the plan. Don't fret if your schedule requires some tweaking to make it the best it can be. Each adjustment brings you one step nearer where you want to be. Praise God you are moving in the right direction, choice by choice, change by change, under the direction of God in heaven. He has the answer to every dilemma or perplexity you may have. He has a way of escape for every difficulty. Trust Him for all your solutions.

Avoid becoming too rigid. A tree that cannot flex is broken in the storm. So, too, does the schedule that is too rigid when confronted by the storm of a child's stubborn will. Dealing with these problems takes time. Remember the schedule is your tool, not your master.

Our skeletons give stability and consistency to our movements. The muscles, tendons and flesh give greater mobility, agility, and grace for us to perform complicated movements in conjunction with the skeleton. With the schedule as our skeleton, we can perform complicated movements in housekeeping, character development, our walk with God, or any goal. Now let's look at fleshing out my *afternoon* schedule.

1:00 P.M.   School subject
2:00 P.M.   School subject
2:30 P.M.   Mother or responsible child—meal preparation
3:00 P.M.   Supper
4:00 P.M.   Kitchen cleanup
5:00 P.M.   Personal time—if all the school work is done well
6:30 P.M.   Family fun time
7:30 P.M.   Personal time
8:00 P.M.   Family worship
8:30 P.M.   Bedtime tuck in

1:00 P.M. After noon break, we resumed school and followed the set pattern of the morning. I continued with my tasks while providing instruction or administering spelling tests, etc. I found I could do all sorts of things, even iron or make bread, in the midst of school. If a subject didn't consume the whole hour, the boys could do something unfinished from the morning classes or have some recess time outside. Remember, my schedule is an example of what we did. You need to do what is best for your family, not just reproduce our plan.

2:00 P.M. Another school subject was done as before. Life's trials and perplexities are the school of Christ to teach us not to murmur or complain. When math or some other subject doesn't go right, we need to teach our children about the powerful, personal God that can save them. This is the most important education we can give our children.

2:30 P.M. While I began or completed my meal preparations for the day, the boys continued at school. When they finished their lessons, they often helped me by making a salad or dessert for supper.

I always had my meals planned out well ahead of time. When my boys got older and took over meal preparation, we made sure that planning ahead and making the grocery list were part of their education. When the boys were ten and twelve, they took over the entire meal preparation, each one being in charge every third day. It was wonderful! It helped them exercise the skills of organization, dispatch, and timeliness—the very skills they would someday need in business. And the free time I gained gave me more time with God and helped my attitude soar and my frustrations diminish even more. It also gave me more time for Jim, which he dearly appreciated, and more time to play with my boys.

3:00 P.M. This was our supper hour. We had pleasant conversation, and it became a very endearing family time. We laughed and showed interest in what each other was doing or thinking. When Jim or I would see a sad expression, we would draw out the problem and find a solution. We tried, not always successfully, to maintain every family member's hold on Jesus throughout the day, for you see, a family approach is the most balanced and most successful when all are following Christ.

4:00 P.M. Kitchen cleanup was the same as before. At the boys' request, we gave one boy dish cleanup for breakfast, while the other cleared the table—and then reversed it at the evening meal. The son who started breakfast dishes would do that for one week. Sometimes there would be a larger amount of dishes for certain meals, and the boys felt this switch balanced out the amount of work. Every family will have their quirks. Enjoy accommodating where you can.

5:00 P.M. After cleanup was accomplished and the house was all in order came personal time. My boys were always involved in one project or another, be it building birdhouses, a bicycle obstacle course, a new path in the woods, or a log jungle gym. Sometimes they just enjoyed simple sports like cross country skiing, hiking, and exploring. The joy of productivity, a job well done, and becoming skillful were their own satisfaction and reward.

If school work was not completed, work duties were not performed at their proper time, or consequences for a bad attitude were necessary, the boys might lose personal time in order to pick up those dropped stitches and make those wrongs right. Losing personal time was a natural consequence for not being cooperative at the right time. With Christ in this equation, it worked wonderful reform.

6:30 P.M. If it's done properly and with Jesus, family fun time is the joy of every child, old or young. In the heart of every child is a desire to be loved and appreciated by his parents. Doing fun activities on a consistent basis will win the hearts of your children and bind them to you unless you are critical, negative, or too exacting.

We had two physically active boys, so we did active things. Your family may be different. You may have other activities that fit your setting, personality, and tastes better. Be creative. Experiment with different ideas to see what works best for your family. God is your ultimate Leader. Follow Him.

7:30 P.M. This was our time to unwind from the day. Sometimes reading filled this period. Often this was my time for a nice soak in the tub, as Jim watched, read to, or played with the children. Ladies, if you have a spouse who is helpful and supportive, thank God and count your blessings. Tell your husband how much you appreciate him, and do so often.

8:00 P.M. Time for family worship once again. The same kind of worship activities are followed as in the morning. Even the very young can be a part of the reading. The parent reads a phrase or sentence, and the little one recites it back. In this way they "read" their verse or paragraph like the big people. Even our little ones can make God's Word practical. They are so open and honest. You will be thrilled to hear what they think. We always made it a point to hug the boys and each other after each worship time. It became a tradition for us and still is to this day.

8:30 P.M. Time for bed can be a very happy and fulfilling time. One more trip to the bathroom, and we all go up to bed. Tucking in our boys was fun. When I kissed my boys on the cheek, they'd be all giggly or they'd try to hide. On occasion we'd have special prayer there at their bedside. I wish we had done more of that when they were little—and even older. The special nature of those times and later the talks with our boys at bedtime leads me to think they are never too old to tuck in. I've talked with fourteen-year-old girls who long still for their parents to tuck them in. Be sensitive to God to lead you to see your children's real needs. Give them time, consistency, and you!

So do your priorities match your schedule? Do you get all the important things in? Does God get the best hours? Where do your spouse and children fit in? Do they have the priority they deserve? When it is all said and done, the only thing on this earth that brings any real pleasure is a personal walk with God. When you have taken the time to develop that walk and talk with Him, when your children have been trained to come to Him as well and are changed in heart, disposition, and character, no greater pleasure exists. When all is right between you and God, between you and your children, you will have peace though the heavens fall. If you substitute anything else in God's place, it will not satisfy. God must become our priority, and our schedules should reflect this choice.

THE LONE EMBRACE
A WORD OF ENCOURAGEMENT FOR SINGLE PARENTS

Scheduling may seem like just another task on your already too-stressed time. But this job will pay you back many times the time invested. No one is more pressed for time than a single parent, and no one benefits more when the children help in a regular and dependable manner.

Change is hard, but remember as the branch grafts into the vine, so we connect with God fiber by fiber, choice by choice, until we are His entirely! Christ desires to become the center of our lives, empowering us to be His sons and daughters. What a joy awaits us all.

Chapter 10

THOUGHTS, FEELINGS, EMOTIONS

"Casting down imaginations, and every high thing that exalteth itself against the knowledge of God, and bringing into captivity every thought to the obedience of Christ" (2 Corinthians 10:5).

Angry gray clouds hung menacingly overhead and reflected their hostility in the churning waters of the North Fork of the Flathead River. It made the wilderness seem even colder as we drove up the North Fork Road, that fifty-mile stretch of dirt and gravel that provides access to our wilderness home. The old truck rattled as we negotiated an endless sea of potholes and ruts. Under the best of conditions, the road is poor, and these were not the best of conditions! The road had been through a number of cycles of freezing and thawing, and ruts had formed, dragging the truck this way and that as we bounced across them.

We have fallen in love with the wilderness. But like anything worth having, wilderness life comes at a high price, and we were still surviving on the equity from our years in Wisconsin. Our budget for luxury items, such as new tires, was non-existent. Jim was driving us home from town on bald tires. With ice coating the road surface and our poor tires, the truck slid toward the outer edge of the road whenever he took a curve. On my side of the truck is the wild, beautiful North Fork River—at the bottom of a steep drop-off with, incidentally, no guardrails! We were high above the river, and when the truck lurched to my side of the road—the river side—my life flashed before me. Soon the "What might happen if . . .?" thoughts began to grip me. "Lord, should I tell Jim he is driving too fast?" the panic was rising fast in my heart.

"No Sally, he is doing just fine for him. This may not be the speed you could drive it, but for him, it's fine. Drivers differ."

I reluctantly accepted the Lord's answer and tried to think about something else. By the time we were halfway home, my emotions were particularly sensitive. More times than I could count, I had been taken to the edge of the road for a view of the river that was just too intimate for my liking. "Lord, what would happen if this truck went over the bank? It would probably break all my bones. It would hurt terrible, wouldn't it? He's driving too fast for me! I'm uncomfortable; I must say something!"

"Because you feel uncomfortable, does that make Jim wrong?"

"Well, no. He can handle the truck; we've never gotten into an accident. He is a good driver. Better than I am. I can trust him."

Just then, Jim took another curve giving me another view of the river. Impulsively, I said, "Jim, are you all right?" What I really meant was, "Are you in control?"

"Yes, I'm all right, honey," he replied calmly, seemingly unaware of my incipient panic.

"Lord, can I tell him to slow down?" I inquired anxiously. "I know I need to filter my thoughts through you before I speak. But I urgently feel the need to tell him. Surely, I wouldn't feel this strongly unless it was right."

"No, Sally, he doesn't need to slow down."

"Then what do I do, Lord, with all this nervousness? It's driving me crazy. I'm so afraid. And try as I may, I don't seem able to control it."

It was the voice of my flesh pushing and compelling me to be anxious, to blame Jim for my feelings, and in turn become irritable with him. The voice of the Spirit tried to encourage me, telling me that everything is all right, while my wrong thoughts and feelings were pushing me—compelling me—to obey them and not God. Changing masters meant letting God have the throne of my heart, which are my thoughts and feelings.

Was the issue Jim's driving? Or my need for Christ to redeem me from my wrong thoughts and feelings? Having Jim slow down to my comfort zone was neither the problem, nor the solution. The issue was: What does God want *me* to do right now? The problem wasn't "If my husband would just . . ." or "If my children would just . . ." or "If my job was just . . ." or "If my home was just . . ." In this and in every situation, the issue is "What are my problems that God wants to fix to bring me peace in Him?" We don't gain peace by controlling the circumstances and everyone around us to our comfort level.

God began to direct my steps, reasoning with me further. *"You know that ninety percent of what you worry about never happens."*

"Yes, that's true! But it doesn't change my feelings. What do I do with them?"

"You need to begin by relaxing and giving those wrong feelings to Me."

"Relax! I could if I weren't taking this near-death ride! Relax? Well, my shoulders are a bit tight." I wiggled my shoulders. Another curve came right then, and I tightened up again, grabbing the door handle, prepared to go over the cliff!

"Are all your worries and fears helping you?" God asked. *"Do you want to continue in them? Just as you have been yielding to these unrighteous fears and thoughts, even so, if you choose, you can yield to right thoughts and feelings."* (See Romans 6:19.)

"So you want me to stop being anxious and worrying about what might happen? I know You can do anything, but it seems so unreal right now. The wrong thoughts and feelings are so much louder than Your voice! I know it's better to be relaxed in an accident—you get hurt less. Besides I don't like all these nervous feelings. I suppose it's logical to stop worrying and being anxious. Lord, my wrong thoughts and feelings are Yours. Take them away. Create a clean heart in me, Lord, and renew a right spirit within me. What should I think on instead?"

"Think trusting thoughts," the Lord encouraged me.

In my mind, I started singing: "Trust and obey, for there is no other way." I paused a moment and then went on trying to puzzle out this whole process. "The Bible says You are the Lord of all flesh and that nothing is too hard for You. It also says perfect love casts out all fear." Just repeating these familiar Scripture promises seemed to have a calming effect in my mind. My hands still clutched the truck door, but the Lord had plans for that too.

"Why are you clutching the door?" God asked gently.

"Oh, do You want me to let go of that, too?" I didn't want to let go. "Hanging onto the door handle won't save me, even in an accident, but hanging onto Jesus will," I reasoned. "It's hard to go against these thoughts and feelings." Finally, I let go of the door handle and relaxed quietly in my seat with my hands folded, clinging to Jesus in my mind. Just about then, we hit another curve, and I instinctively grabbed the door handle again.

"It's okay, Sally," the Lord prompted me. Again, I made the choice to let go of the door and resumed my new position.

Bit by bit, as I continually surrendered around each curve, the emotions subsided. They were gone before we reached home. This wasn't a one-time victory. God gave me a chance to practice on every trip to town! But as I repeated these choices, the fear became less and my trust in Jesus grew. The process always began in my thoughts. If I indulged "What if . . .?" thoughts, it was harder. If I decided right away to trust and not worry, it was easier. The process of choice and cooperation with God gave me freedom. Soon there were no more worries or fears in my heart! And we never did have an accident with those bald tires! Praise God!

Do you see how God directed my reason in order to free me? At the time, I couldn't see beyond the crisis of conflicting emotions or explain what God was doing. In reflective time, though, I began to understand that God could not redeem me until I cooperated with Him in my thoughts. Yet He never forced me to do things His way. Only as I gave Him permission to work in me could He re-create my feelings so that they were in harmony with His thoughts and will. This is what the Bible is talking about when it says, "bringing into captivity every thought to the obedience of Christ" (2 Corinthians 10:5).

God wants our hearts which, in essence, are our thoughts and feelings. God is most interested in developing His character in us. Our characters are our thoughts and feelings combined. These drive our emotions, inclinations, responses, habits, desires, and passions. So when God has our thoughts and feelings, He has all of us. That is why the sin battle is a battle for the mind. This is why the text, "Let this mind be in you . . ." (Philippians 2:5), is so basic to what a Christian truly is. The battle between good and evil is the battle to determine what thoughts and feeling we choose to let rule us. Only through the power found in Christ can we serve God and right in the inner man.

What if I hadn't cooperated with God and chosen to think right thoughts? I would have been bound tighter in the cords of bondage to my fears. When anxiety is pushing and ruling me, I can *claim* to belong to God, but do I really? I can fake it, but that doesn't alter my true condition. I am still a slave to my fears—and to Satan. The same is true of other harmful emotions—irritation, envy, jealousy, hatred, or the snippy spirit that comes out unexpectedly. You see, we may deceive others for a time, but we are the only ones fooled in the long run. We may think we are loving Christians, yet if we react hatefully to those who cross us, demonstrate a pushy spirit, or become domineering, we are not Christ's at all. What we do says more about whom we serve than what we say. "Even a child is known by his doings, whether his work be pure, and whether it be right" (Proverbs 20:11).

We don't have to obey the perverted demands of our sinful human natures. Appetites, feelings, and desires are not wrong in and of themselves. However, they may disagree with God's way. And when they do, we need to take them to God to be changed.

Whatever is in us that does not agree with God's way needs to be given to Him to be subdued. And in its place we need to do whatever God directs us to do. Often God asks us to cultivate thoughts and deeds that have opposite traits to those He wants to remove from our lives—happiness for sadness or love for hate.

God is ever sending messages to His people, and we hinder Him by refusing the thoughts that He brings to our mind. We discard them without first considering whether they might truly be from God. Why? Perhaps because they seem ridiculous. Or perhaps we want to put off making a decision. Or because we don't want to have to examine ourselves.

Often we feel so inadequate and unworthy we can't believe that God would possibly speak to *us!* This terribly hinders God's ability to communicate with us. If we believe He will not help us, we truly become helpless because without God, we are incapable of lasting changes. Satan has studied the human mind and knows that the best way to keep us from God is to plant lying thoughts in our minds, especially thoughts rooted in our fears and doubts. These thoughts push us into wrong habits and attitudes, which in turn, prompt us to do wrong things and thus produce guilt! If you're like me, guilt tends to send you running *from* God, not *to* Him. Satan laughs at our condition, knowing that in this weakened state it will be increasingly hard for us to exercise faith and almost impossible to believe that God loves and accepts us in spite of our faults. Thus Satan keeps us captive.

There is a way to break free from the trap of wrong thinking. The good news is that your freedom can begin today—if you will only choose to believe and take God at His word. God has placed in every person the precious freedom to choose, and Satan cannot take this from you. He may intimidate you, he may stir up your rotten feelings and emotions, but he cannot make you believe his lies! It is left with us to apply our will to cooperate with these things. When we take God at His word instead of believing Satan's lying thoughts, we will have victory!

The choice starts in our minds. We can choose to surrender to God and His will, believing that His way is right and best. This choice must take place before our actions will ever change. God longs to redeem us and set us free, but until we surrender and give Him control, He cannot.

The next step is to act on whatever He tells us to do, no matter how simple or how little it seems to make sense. If we do this, redemptive love begins to flow into our habits, inclinations, and emotions to transform them. Let's look at how this works in real life.

I *love* cookies! I was born with a *big* sweet tooth. I could never eat just *one* cookie. But I became a Christian and was learning to listen to God. One day I was washing dishes and snacking on cookies. I had just finished my first cookie and automatically reached for a second—and then a third. But God broke into my thoughts. *"Sally, you don't need another cookie. Two cookies are enough."*

"It doesn't really matter if I have more than two; they're small," I responded. Then I stopped. "Lord, is that You? I *have* been asking You to help me not overeat."

"Yes, Sally, I'm here with you to help you overcome, if you wish. In Me you can choose to say "no" to the cookies. You've had enough."

Every fiber of my being rebelled at this idea, and yet I knew I had to decide! My mind flipped back and forth. "I want a cookie. I want to obey Jesus. But I really want another cookie!" I looked at the third cookie in my hand. "God is right. If I eat another cookie, I'll eat several more, and soon I'll discover I've eaten half the package." I remembered times I had eaten so many cookies that I worried Jim would find the half-eaten package and know what I had done. So I'd eat the other half—to get rid of the evidence! Of course, I carried around a heavy load of guilt for the next few hours, not to mention an irritable disposition and a very unhappy stomach!

"I don't want to eat another cookie, Lord," I said and put the third cookie back. But if I thought the battle was over, was I ever wrong!

The voice of the tempter popped into my head. "Those cookies are your favorite kind! Just one more isn't going to hurt you! You're mowing the lawn today, so you'll work it all off."

"No. I've decided not to have another cookie!"

"But you're so hungry. You didn't eat much breakfast. You'll never make it until lunch." Just then my stomach growled in agreement!

"Oh, I do want a cookie! No, I don't want another cookie! I want to obey Jesus. Help me, Lord! I feel like I'm starving to death! I know it's ridiculous, but that's how I feel! What should I do?"

"Why don't you go vacuum the living room," the Lord suggested.

"That's a good idea. The carpet doesn't need vacuuming, but I need to do something to get the cookie idea out of my head!" I ran to the closet, pulled out my vacuum, and began vacuuming furiously.

After about five minutes, the Lord prompted me with this thought. *"Do you still want that cookie?"*

When you struggle with appetite as I have, this is a question you simply don't ask because the answer is always, "Of course, I want a cookie! I love cookies! I always want a cookie!" Thinking about them just makes you want them more, and eventually you give in and eat them no matter how far away you hide them! At least I always did!

But this time I sensed something was different. "Is this God?" I wondered. I hesitatingly asked myself the question, "You still want that cookie, don't you?"

My answer surprised me. "No!" The very thought of eating another cookie repulsed me. "This is different," I thought. "It can't be—or can it?" I had to know, so I did something dangerous. I imagined myself eating a cookie, a delicious wonderful cookie. Before, this would always draw me to the cookie package with an almost irresistible force. To my amazement, I didn't start salivating. I wasn't even interested. "Lord, where did my feelings go? What have You done? I'm free! This is amazing! I don't even want to eat a cookie!" What a joy!

When we give God our thoughts and feelings, He will bring all our desires under His control and win the battle for us. He is a wonderful God who longs to free us from serving sin. Our history of failure doesn't matter. Our weaknesses don't matter. He is strong enough for all our needs.

And when we understand how to cooperate with God, then we can teach our children to do the same. What a wonderful opportunity to unite His divine presence to our human effort! God is able—and through Him, so are we!

THE LONE EMBRACE
A SPECIAL WORD OF ENCOURAGEMENT FOR SINGLE PARENTS

As a single parent you may feel that you have good reason to feel emotionally devastated. Many of you have told me, "You don't understand what it's like to be a single parent." Perhaps that is so, but the process for dealing with painful emotions and wrong thought patterns is the same for all of us. Your situation may be terribly unfair, but God has planted within your heart the ability to choose the type of life you will lead and the level of happiness you will experience.

One of the hardest things to do is to allow someone else—a former spouse or even our own children—to be happy when we are feeling miserable. We tend to see our unhappiness as a direct outgrowth of another's actions. "If he hadn't done that or if she would only act differently, then I wouldn't be so sad." But, as I learned on that long drive home over icy roads, perception is not always truth. No one can rob you of your peace of mind and happiness unless you allow it. Your situation is doubtless difficult, and although you can't change the past, you *can*—through the power of Christ—change your present!

Chapter 11

THE JOYS OF MOTHERHOOD

"To [God] be glory and dominion for ever and ever. Amen" (Revelation 1:6).

*M*oments of time have formed the book of our lives. As we review its pages, seldom can we do so without pangs of regret for what we might have done, what we should have said, or the path we could have followed with better results. As a mother, I certainly haven't done everything perfectly. Far from it. Many things I would do differently if I could. Yet, by God's grace, I have few regrets. Under Christ's leadership, I've received what I most desired—a well-ordered, well-disciplined, Christ-centered family. Surely there is no greater reward on earth.

When we moved from Wisconsin to Montana, we sacrificed our careers and the potential for financial prosperity. We left behind all the advantages of life in suburbia. But we also knew that all the sacrifice would be worthwhile if we could somehow make finding God our top priority. The move was truly a faith step. Our friends thought we were crazy. Our families didn't understand. Even our church family thought we had become fanatical. At that time, we couldn't have explained exactly what we were going to do—because we didn't know ourselves! Jim and I chose to follow God and to let the results demonstrate if this was His will. There were good, logical reasons *not* to do what we did, but those who voiced such reasoning didn't understand that we were desperate enough to risk anything, if only we could find that which we desired.

On one of our first exploratory walks in Montana, we found ourselves in a large, open field. The July sun warmed the tall grass. Tiny flowers added their perfume to the pleasant smell of pine and the beauty of the glacial river. Matthew and Andrew took one look and began running amid this scene of beauty, a perfect image of freedom, hemmed in only by their parents' love and the grandeur of the Rocky Mountains in the distance. Jim and I marveled at the spectacle before us, savoring the sight of our boys exploring the tall grass in a huge open field with huge smiles of pure glee on their faces. It was hard to avoid the feeling that this was the way we were meant to live, that this was, in fact, the way all humans were designed to live. Oh what a delight to our senses! What a contrast to our former life in the city suburbs. Our boys would be safe here!

In our new life we could tell the boys, "Yes, let's go for a walk. Daddy doesn't have to go to work today." We could say, "Yes, let's go for a mountain hike, and when we get to the top, we have the time to swim in the lake." "Yes, let's build something together." "Yes, I have time to read you a book." In the old life, something else always had priority. In the mountains, we had no work, no phone, nothing that was more important than our family. Our children really want only us. They don't need or want many toys if they can have us!

Jim and I were free too! Free to follow God as we felt He wanted us to. Free to adjust our schedules, free to place God first, last, and best. Free to be the new people we were becoming, rather than who we had been. We fell in love with each other, and our boys with us, as we never could have in our former lifestyle. For one whole year, I kept asking Jim, "Do we really live here or is this just a dream that I'll wake up from all too soon?"

Jim joined in helping me raise our sons. This had long been my wish, for I knew I couldn't handle them myself. He became their friend, teaching them how to play and teaching me how to run the home like a business. I thrived. The boys thrived. And Jim, who perhaps had the hardest transition to make, also thrived, eventually becoming the leader of our family not only in work and play but also in spiritual things. He led by teaching real-life, practical spiritual lessons. I admire him so much for that because the habits he instilled in our boys have never left them. Today our boys are married, and we see them conducting their own family worships—leading out and promoting discussion, just like Jim does. What we showed them in our home, they have reproduced in their own homes, each according to his personality and individual creative flair.

Such a result doesn't just happen. It is the natural outgrowth of the life and influences their parents have chosen for them, and we didn't have to wait until they were adults to see the seeds taking root in their hearts. Some years after we moved to the mountains, our boys were playing outside one fall evening, sitting atop the crossbars of their jungle gym. In their innocent joy, they began singing hymns and Christmas carols at the top of their lungs. Then they sang with great feeling, "Jesus loves me this I know . . ." They sang not just because it was a familiar song; they sang because they had come to know from experience that Jesus truly did love them. It brought tears to both Jim and me. What we were trying to do was working. It was really working! The key ingredient was letting God lead and direct our steps. All our former choices—some of them very hard choices, involving much self-denial on our part—had brought us to this place, and we realized in that moment that to have peace in our hearts and to bond our children's hearts to God, nothing is too costly.

Schooling my boys at home was a real challenge. Yet, God leading, we not only got through school, but the boys excelled. Home school crossed the wills of every member of our family, but by the time the boys were ten and twelve years of age, all the hard work was paying off with great dividends. They didn't just know *about* God, they had found Him a personal Friend in trials. They knew the voice of God speaking to their hearts and minds. They recognized temptations, and they were discovering in the Word of God the practical arts of surrender and cooperation. While they did this, I was learning that, in Jesus, I was capable of success even in areas difficult for me—and I rejoiced.

Once the routine of school was established, the heart work understood and entered into, the boys' wills engaged, and study habits underway, home schooling turned into a beautiful, desirable experience. Instead of problems with the will, trials, and figuring out strategies, we developed team efforts to face our wrongs. All this brought forth the fruit of good learning, excellent grades, and freedom from self-will ruling in the life.

We had the boys tested periodically by a school representative, and this proved we were indeed mastering the educational basics better than I had hoped. But still I strove for excellence, desiring them to be the best they could be in Jesus. At the completion of their education, they took their GED exams, and to my joy, they scored in the 97th to 98th percentile nationwide. This is not to my glory, but to God's.

At fourteen and sixteen years of age the boys were working in construction and went into that work full time shortly thereafter. Both hired on with Coldwell Banker as independent real estate agents when they turned eighteen. They grew and became quite successful in their business, becoming respected for their honest and forthright business practices. One day their hard work and economy paid off when they could purchase their own first car without any debt!

My boys are men today—successful in their chosen fields of real estate. Looking at them now, I think back to the early lessons that have proved such a blessing, lessons that have given them their ability to work, to carry responsibilities through to completion, and to find joy in a job well done. Many of those lessons came from learning to carry their share of the practical household duties. They learned to run the house as well as I did, and their father taught them the manly outdoor skills until they rivaled him in quality and speed.

The reason they helped so much was to free up my time. For a mother, the joy of having time to play with her children is very special. Sad to say, many mothers are slaves to their homes or their occupations, and the children get crowded out for lack of time. I loved playing with my children. I just didn't think it possible until I found out what good workers I had right under my feet! Mothers desperately need play time, too. We need time to have fun, enjoy life, and be kids ourselves.

By investing in the hard lessons of self-denial and by pouring time and energy into our children, we saw the teen years slip by without the rebellious, uncooperative attitudes so commonly seen in those years. Teens do not rebel just because they are biologically programmed to. The teen years are not something that simply must be endured. Although every child must make the difficult transition to adulthood, many more could do so without major conflict if parents would act as encouraging coaches, raising their children God's way, not their way. If I'm being fair and honest, if I am not dominating, if I have learned self-control—and teach my children these same lessons God is teaching me—He is able to give them self-control through His Spirit. The teen years don't have to be such a difficult experience as far too many parents and teens have had to suffer through.

One of the ways we survived back when money was tight was to maintain a large garden and a greenhouse in which we grew as much of our food as possible. Of course, all these growing plants had their own needs for warmth, water, and nourishment; so that only the combined efforts of our whole family allowed us to enjoy the bounty of the earth at harvest. Our children learned about responsibility in a situation where everyone had to pull his own weight, with the full and certain knowledge that his faithfulness would have a direct impact upon our table.

Fruit we couldn't grow ourselves, we bought in bulk and canned hundreds of quarts every year. The boys and I were hard workers and didn't allow these tasks to take longer than necessary. Quickness and efficiency were our goals, and we improved every year. But the greatest joy was when Jim would join us canning. He always made it extra fun! One year, he joined us in canning cherries and turned it into a race. Oh, such fun! Andrew cleaned; Jim pitted; and Matthew ran back and forth, supplying his father with cherries and bringing me the pitted cherries to process. Jim set a fast pace, and we all scrambled to keep up. We were laughing, working fast, and jostling each other good naturedly as we worked in our small kitchen. My canning kettle could hardly keep up! And best of all was the sight of jars of deep red cherries stacking up on my kitchen counter. Cherry juice was everywhere, but oh, what a joyful memory for all of us! We got the job done in record time, which allowed us to go outside and play baseball. What a joy to learn to balance work and play.

As I write this it was more than a year ago that I watched Matthew and his lovely bride, Angela, walk down the aisle as man and wife. It brought tears to my eyes. God's presence was markedly manifest. The service was heart moving and elegant. Many guests said it was the most spiritual wedding they had ever attended. Everyone commented about the sweet spirit that reigned. Four pastors attended the wedding—two young pastors and two who were retired. They said it was the most spiritual, uplifting wedding they had ever attended. They greatly sensed God's presence. The only complaint we received was that we didn't supply tissues for everyone—especially during Matthew's love song to Angela, "I Will Be There for You." It was heart-wrenching and beautiful.

Matthew and Angela were so special and so right for each other. The two most outstanding memories of that event are Angela's dancing eyes and looks of deep admiration for Matthew and Matthew's heartfelt love song deeply dedicating himself to Angela. After a year and a half of marriage, these two attributes remain in their home. As I launched my son into life as a married man, I began a new phase of my life as a mother. I saw in Matthew's and Angela's relationship a deeper level of compatibility than I had ever seen before. They knew each other's strengths and weaknesses in such detail and found they were compatible even in their weaknesses. Little by little, and deeper and deeper, they fell in love. Even through trials and difficulties, they found themselves bonded ever closer. God showed His approving hand along the way in loving ways. Their courtship was so sweet and pure that it was a thrill to watch. We affectionately called them the "kitties" for their spirited play and tussling.

But Matthew was not my only son to marry in 2002. Andrew and Sarah had an equally special relationship, and God showed His hand in many little ways, approving of their union step by step and year by year. Living twenty-five hundred miles apart, they found their parting more difficult with each separation. Matthew and Angela may have been kitties, but we called Sarah and Andrew the "puppies." They were so sweet and gentle in their play! The story of both weddings is special to me, but I'd like to focus right now on a dream—Sarah's dream. Ever since she was a little girl, Sarah had dreamed of being married outdoors in the fall. So that is what she and Andrew planned, a beautiful wedding out of doors in the mountains of North Carolina.

The foot of Grandfather Mountain was a perfect setting, but Sarah's dream of crisp leaves, bright sunshine, and Indian summer seemed in danger. We arrived on Wednesday in rain that had already set in for most of the week. The rain made it difficult to erect the large tent for the reception area. However, Friday was clear, and hopes soared that the very soggy field would dry out. Sunday, the weather again refused to cooperate. Rain came and went, low clouds covered the mountain, and the forecast predicted an eighty percent chance of rain. We knew God was able to change the weather if He chose, and I can't tell you how fervently we prayed for Him to do so. A wedding is a once-in-a-lifetime event, and every girl should be able to realize her dream on her wedding day.

With the ceremony drawing nearer and no improvement in the weather, Andrew faced an excruciating decision—to set up outside with the risk of rain ruining the service or moving the service inside the large tent. The decision had been put off as long as possible; now, less than two hours before the wedding, it had to be made. To make matters worse, we all knew that Sarah's father wasn't going to be able to sing at her wedding as she had hoped. Ken had practiced the song, but his emotions were too close to the surface. He had choked up and had to get a substitute. "Poor Sarah," I thought, "God, please give this girl, who we have come to love, the desires of her heart." Knowing all about her dream, Andrew glanced one last time at very threatening skies, prayed, and then said, "God can do it; He can do anything. We will trust in God."

Jim leaped for joy at Andrew's decision and commanded, "Set up the chairs outside!"

I heard his voice and immediately joined a throng of well-wishers setting up outside. Everyone knew what a risk this was. Some expressed joy and faith that God was going to give this couple their special day, while others thought it was pure foolishness. As I went to dress, I turned to look back at the field. Mist was coming down, getting the chairs wet, but there was our dear friend Jo Lynn making sure that everything was in its proper place, ignoring the rain, seeing only with the eye of faith. What an encouragement!

While this was going on, Sarah and Angela were driving to the site, the mist wetting the windshield of their car. Sarah asked over and over, "What do you think Andrew decided? Inside or outside? Inside or out?" She had left the choice to him, trusting his judgment. Outside was her dream, but everything around her told her to not get her hopes up and let go of her dream.

Angela could see how forlorn the situation looked and couldn't bring herself to offer much encouragement in the face of the rain. "I don't know, Sarah," was all she could bring herself to reply, "but we'll soon see for ourselves." As they crested the last hill, a delightful little scream broke the silence as Sarah cried out, "He set up outside! He set up outside!"

Meanwhile, Ken had told me that he had decided he *was* going to sing. He made arrangements with the vocalist to accompany him. "Oh Ken," I burst out, "you will make your daughter so happy! This means a lot to her. God will be with you! In Him, you can sing without breaking down! This is a real privilege. I'll be praying for you! Just remember, God can keep you, Ken!"

Andrew seated me and gave me a surprise kiss, his last kiss as a single man. For me, it was a dream come true. I hadn't expected that. Oh, how I wish I had a picture of his kiss! Then the service began, and Jim said, "Andrew and Sarah, look up and see your first wedding present. God gave you the gift of the sun on your wedding day. He can do anything. Isn't He wonderful?"

Sure enough, miracle of miracles, the mountaintop had cleared! Over our heads was a circle of thin white clouds in the center of a larger circle of angry dark gray clouds being held back by unseen angels. Thunder rumbled in the distance, and I couldn't help but think it was Satan, angry that God had said, "This far and no farther, Satan!" The unusual round hole in the center of those angry clouds remained above the field until the wedding was finished, a little more than an hour! It was the most wonderful gift from God to these two for their wedding day! He honored their wedding with His presence as He had honored the wedding at Cana and met real needs. And God wasn't done with surprises for Sarah. God enabled Ken to sing. He did a lovely, well-controlled job—giving his special gift of love in a song to his daughter.

The miracle of the weather was the talk of the rest of the day. Every wish and dream of Sarah's was fulfilled this day—the outdoor wedding, the sunshine, the mountain views, the fall colors, and her father singing. Oh how lovely to live out your dreams together in God's power! At the reception, a man came to Jim and told him that he had thought we were really foolish to set up in the mist with the forecast such as it was. "But," he continued, "after what happened today, I believe in Andrew's God." Another person told Sarah, "This weather was a real miracle. I want to ask you to pray for me because you obviously have a direct line to heaven." He didn't seem to understand that everyone can claim God's blessings—just not everyone does.

Still others said this miracle at the wedding was like the parting of the sea for Israel. The Israelites had to step in before the waters parted. God's parting of the storm was His way of honoring this wedding. We all go through storms in our day-to-day life. We need to see God's miracles in our storms as we cry out to Him to bring the sunshine. All the lessons learned came to fruition that day when Andrew took his step of faith—not sight. All of us who are parents have the blessed privilege and high calling of giving to the next generation the inheritance of knowing a personal God whom they can trust.

I can't speak firsthand of fatherhood, and although I have tremendous respect for Jim and the job he has done, I know his struggles differed from mine as a mother. You see, motherhood is perhaps the ultimate giving of yourself. It begins the moment that newly formed embryo takes its life from you and never ends throughout the years. It is caring for and loving a child when you are too tired to care for yourself. It is doing for your child that which you would never do for your own sake. Motherhood is endless work, endless worry, endless problems, and challenges beyond human ability or capacity. The hardest thing about motherhood is seeing yourself reflected at your very worst in your children. Motherhood is the hardest job anyone can perform—and yet the most important.

Motherhood is a baby's first smile, his first steps, and his first successes. It is the joy of little hugs, of dirty faces, and precious gifts of crushed dandelions. It is the excitement and high adventure of exploration, the satisfaction of experiencing the new skills and interests of an expanding mind, and the thrill of seeing spiritual awakening in your child. Motherhood is watching the man or the woman growing within the child and the thrill of watching judgment mature. Motherhood is seeing your "baby" walk down the aisle; it's watching a new generation begin. Motherhood is so many things that are difficult and unpleasant, and yet motherhood is everything left in this world that is good, kind, loving, and noble. In the end, motherhood is hearing Christ say, "Well done, thou good and faithful servant" and seeing God place the crown of life upon the head of your children.

True motherhood requires an active faith and a dependence upon a God who longs to work miracles for you and for your child, a God who desires, more than anything else, to lift your burdens and help you in your efforts for your little ones.

The only question remaining is: "Will you let God part the clouds of heaven for you and live to raise your precious ones to walk with Him?"

Sally and Matthew, 1977—the joy of being a mother!

Jim and Matthew, 1979.

The only survivor of three bear cubs became our family pet!

Matthew at two years old with Andrew at the time he was having so much colic.

Matthew in the sandbox from which he wandered away and was lost!

Our place in Wisconsin where Matthew wandered away from home and became lost when he was two years old. This aerial view shows just how miraculous it was that we found him safe and unharmed.

Backpacking as a family has been one of the blessings of living in the mountains.

Wedding giggles! Matthew's and Angela's wedding, August 11, 2002.

Andrew and Sarah's wedding, 2002. God performed a miracle to hold back the storm and preserve Sarah's dream of an outdoor ceremony in the mountains!

New from Jim Hohnberger!

Come to the Quiet

Leaving a life of material comforts and dead spirituality in Wisconsin, Jim and Sally Hohnberger took up their search for an intimate life with God on a remote property in the Montana wilderness. In this book Jim provides new details and lessons not included in *Escape to God*. If your life is inundated with phone calls, e-mails, meetings, the expectations of others, and an endless list of things to do, you need to Come to the Quiet—the quiet of resting in Jesus. This book shows you how.

0-8163-2032-2. Paperback.
US$13.99, Can$20.99.

Other best-selling books from Jim Hohnberger

It's About People

In what may be his most important book yet, Jim Hohnberger attempts to reconcile the faith we preach with the gospel we live—when we disagree. Jim shows how Jesus' attitude and approach towards those who didn't receive Him was just as important as the truth He taught.

0-8163-1964-2. Paperback.
US$10.99, Can$16.49.

Empowered Living

A thoughtful collection of principles and testimonies of how God can revolutionize your marriage, family, and your walk with God.

0-8163-1917-0. Paperback.
US$14.99, Can$22.49.

Escape to God

How the Hohnberger family left the rat race behind to search for genuine spirituality and the simple life.

0-8163-1805-0. Paperback.
US$13.99, Can$20.99

Order from your ABC by calling **1-800-765-6955**, or get online and shop our virtual store at **www.adventistbookcenter.com**.
- Read a chapter from your favorite book
- Order online
- Sign up for email notices on new products

For more information on the Hohnberger's ministry or other materials call 1-877-755-8300 or www.EmpoweredLivingMinistries.org.